Jermain Defoe

The Biography

Michael Perkin

JOHN BLAKE

Published by John Blake Publishing Ltd,
3 Bramber Court, 2 Bramber Road,
London W14 9PB, England

www.johnblakepublishing.co.uk

First published in hardback in 2010

ISBN: 978-1-84358-252-6

British Library Cataloguing-in-Publication Data:

A catalogue record for this book is available from the British Library.

Design by www.envydesign.co.uk

Printed in Great Britain by CPI William Clowes, Beccles, NR34 7TL

1 3 5 7 9 10 8 6 4 2

Papers used by John Blake Publishing are natural, recyclable products made from
wood grown in sustainable forests. The manufacturing processes conform to the
environmental regulations of the country of origin.

Every attempt has been made to contact the relevant copyright-holders,
but some were unobtainable. We would be grateful if the appropriate
people could contact us.

For Mum, Dad and Sarah
Thank you for all your love
and encouragement

Contents

Contents

Acknowledgements

I would like to thank Nick Callow and all at Hayters Teamwork for the opportunity they have given me, as well as their guidance and advice.

I am also grateful to Allie Collins at John Blake Publishing for all the hard work and organisation that has gone into putting this book together.

None of this would have been possible without the endless love and support from my family and friends. I thank my family for telling me when to knuckle down and work hard, and my friends for telling me when not to.

Introduction

Not many players have scored five goals in a single Premier League game. In fact, before the 2009/10 season, only two had managed the feat. When Jermain Defoe took to the field for Tottenham Hotspur against Wigan Athletic on a chilly November afternoon, very little was expected other than a home win. But in the space of 40 second-half minutes the nimble front man had powered his way into the record books with a quintuple of his own as Spurs made history with a 9-1 victory. It was a fine achievement – but it said it all that not many people in the game were surprised.

Making history is something Defoe has become famous for and is the reason why, at the age of just 27, he is a regular in the Premier League for Tottenham Hotspur, a regular member of the England squad and one of the most prominent strikers in English football today. His goal return in the top flight of English football continues to get better, but that is something that many people have come to expect since he burst onto the professional scene as a teenager. His ability to equal records and make a name for himself at the highest level is testament to his hard work and his desire to make his dreams come true.

After learning his trade as a boy at Charlton, Defoe raised a few eyebrows when he signed professional forms at West Ham. But a loan spell at Bournemouth alerted the football world to what he was capable of on the pitch rather than what he was doing off it. Goals in ten consecutive league games led him to be mentioned in the same breath as such English scoring sensations as John Aldridge and Dixie Dean, and even the greatest striker of them all, Pelé. Just like the legendary Brazilian, Defoe was a hit at 17 years of age. And that was only the beginning of the inspiring story of this young lad from east London.

He might not be the biggest, but Defoe's pace and astounding ability to find the back of the net with a rocket of a shot from either foot meant the physical side of the game was never much of a problem. He had all the attributes necessary to make it in the Premier League, and he showed that by finishing as West Ham's top scorer in his first full season, despite being used almost exclusively as a substitute. Even after the Hammers were relegated the following year, he maintained his desire to perform as well as he could and his goals in the Football League earned him a move back to the top flight at Tottenham.

His performances at White Hart Lane during the mid-2000s impressed then England manager Sven-Göran Eriksson, who gave Defoe a full debut in 2004 against Poland in a World Cup qualifier. The striker showed he was ready for the rigours of international football with a goal on his first England start.

In fact, debut goals have been something of a speciality for Defoe, offering another reason for him to go down in football folklore. He has managed the feat for England at under-21 and senior level, as well as at every club he has played for.

Defoe had his ups and downs in his first stint at White Hart Lane and despite controversially missing out on a place in the England squad for the 2006 World Cup, he showed he could overcome adversity, just as he'd had to do when West Ham were relegated. He was able to bounce back from disappointment as well as any player, and he would need that strength of character when he fell out of favour at Spurs.

One man who has played a pivotal role in Defoe's story, and continues to do so, is Harry Redknapp. The manager who gave Defoe his first taste of professional football at West Ham came to the striker's rescue with a lifeline at Portsmouth. It was there that Defoe was first given the opportunity to lead the line in the Premier League. Alongside his friend and future Tottenham and England ally Peter Crouch, Defoe would become one of the most feared strikers in the top flight. It came as little surprise that when Redknapp moved on to Spurs he took both men with him – Defoe for the hefty price of £15 million.

It was his fine form in his second spell at Tottenham that enabled Defoe to achieve his ultimate dream – to play for his country at a World Cup finals. He was picked by Fabio Capello to play for England in South Africa in the summer of 2010. The tournament did not go to plan for the national team, but Defoe was one of the few bright sparks, with his dramatic winning goal against Slovenia sending England into the knockout stages of the competition. Another dream realised.

Jermain Defoe has already achieved so much before the age of 30. He has not yet reached the peak of his powers in footballing terms but already he is a household name. He has set himself some daunting standards, but if he can continue to meet them as he has done so far, then he can continue to make his dreams come true. The story of his career has been a fascinating one, with joy, despair, elation and tragedy along the way. He has come through so much with flying colours already, and there is still so much more to come.

Chapter 1

Childhood

Jermain Colin Defoe was born on 7 October 1982 to parents Sandra and Jimmy in Beckton, east London. However, it was with his mother that the future England star would forge much the stronger relationship. Sandra was just 18 when she gave birth to Jermain, and his upbringing was not the easiest. Jimmy left the family when his son was only three years old, leaving the job of raising and nurturing him to his mother and his West Indian grandmother Mary. It was thanks to these two strong and loving women that young Jermain would develop the strong sense of family unity that would be prevalent in all his endeavours – from school to church to the football pitch.

Defoe readily admits that his early years were difficult for his family. Still a teenager, Sandra had her own life to lead and despite being full of love, support and pride for her son, she left much of the early work of raising him to her mother, a lady whom Jermain loved dearly and who clearly loved him in return. He revealed to the *Sun* that Mary was like 'a second mum' to him and that they would always spend time together. There was no doubt she knew how to bring up a family in the right way, having worked hard to raise six children herself. In fact Mary often encouraged her grandson to pursue his footballing dreams, although not in her house. 'She used to hide all my balls because I used to smash her light bulbs kicking them about,' Jermain fondly recalled. 'But when she hid my footballs I used to roll my socks into a ball and use that to kick around!' It was pretty clear even then that Defoe would grow up to be a striker.

Living with his mother and grandmother gave the youngster the stability he needed after the departure of his father. It was said that Jimmy's life was influenced heavily by drink and drug problems. He also fathered Jermain's half-brother Jade and had three other sons, all by different women. A source close to Jimmy revealed that his existence was one of 'booze and ambling round betting shops'. He had also been seen at a Crisis shelter soup kitchen near his home in Canning Town, east London – a long way from the sort of lifestyle that his son leads now, but also light years away from the caring family environment in which Defoe was so blessed to grow up.

Much of this would be thanks to the unbending support given to Defoe by his mother. As Sandra matured into a loving single parent she became the focal point of her son's progression from schoolboy to church choirboy to footballer – amateur and professional. A 2009 article in the *Sunday Times* revealed how much she meant, and continues to mean, to him. It was her influence that led Jermain never to drink alcohol, and indeed disobeying her is still something that scares him. In fact, disappointing her in any way by something he has said or done will result in her giving him 'The Look' – something any son close to their mother will do their utmost to avoid.

While Mary offered plenty of help to raise Jermain and take care of him, Sandra worked her absolute hardest to make life for her only son as easy as possible. Modern society might call it a 'broken home', but other than the light bulbs there was nothing broken about the relationship between these three devoted people. Defoe told the *Sunday Times*: 'It was difficult for her... She raised me on her own and raising a son is difficult enough for a woman already. She'd work around the clock to buy me shin pads and football boots.' Proof again that if Jermain was going to become a footballer, then his mum and grandma would support him every step of the way.

In fact, focusing on football seemed to be the best way for Defoe to steer clear of a rough world around him. Growing up on a council estate in Beckton, he was aware of a significant amount of violence taking place on his doorstep. But that was something the football-mad youngster was never involved in. In fact he admitted to using football as something of an escape, even in his teenage years and early professional career. Like any young man he wanted to be out and about with his friends. Not on Mum's watch. 'I always wanted to be out in the square,' said Jermain in 2004. 'Mum would say, especially when I had football training the next day, "You shouldn't be out late – you should rest."'

With all the love and care he received at home, it was little wonder that Defoe was able to thrive on a rich and enjoyable childhood both in school and on the football pitch. His primary education was undertaken at St Joachim Primary

School in nearby Custom House, before he started secondary school at St Bonaventure's Catholic Comprehensive School in Forest Gate, also in east London. It was here that Defoe would start out on the road to his dreams, but against a background of strict religious observance of the Catholic faith – again under the watchful eye of his mother. This was something that would have a profound effect on him in all walks of life.

'She always makes sure I go to church,' Defoe told the *Mirror* in 2006. 'I went to a Catholic primary school and secondary school and I've always enjoyed going to church.' A year later he explained to the *Evening Standard* that he would pray every Sunday and still does, although other commitments prevent him from singing in the church choir nowadays as he did in his youth. He would often go to old people's homes and sing for the residents, another part of his childhood that he remembers with a genuine fondness. The enjoyment he drew from his regular church attendance was the starting point for the much deeper understanding of religion he developed in later life, with prayer becoming a release when football and family matters brought their inevitable difficulties.

For example, when Defoe was surprisingly omitted from Sven-Göran Eriksson's England squad for the 2006 World Cup in favour of Arsenal's untried and untested teenager Theo Walcott, he sought solace in his religious beliefs. Similarly, he looked to prayer the following season when he was struggling to hold down a regular place in the Tottenham starting line-up under manager Martin Jol. Defoe has said that prayer was a huge source of inspiration to him, allowing him to remain thankful for everything he had and offering the opportunity to be thankful again when he returned to form and a place in Jol's starting eleven.

Defoe's religion was also on hand to offer comfort after the tragic loss of his half-brother Jade, who died from a head injury after an alleged attack in Leytonstone in April 2009. Jade had not followed the football route, instead expressing his talent in the music industry. But the two were close, and Jade's death hit this close-knit family hard. It was Defoe's mother who broke the news to him that Jade had not long left, and they would help each other, and the rest of the family, to get through this devastating period in their lives. As Defoe poignantly put it in September 2009: 'Sometimes in life you get difficult times and at some point you get good times. We were a close family so when we heard the news you can imagine what it felt like.' But with the faith instilled in the family by their close bonds and religious belief they have been able to begin moving on and remember Jade in a positive way.

It is clear that for Defoe church is much more than a childhood passing phase. In a world where high-profile professional footballers do not enjoy the best of reputations off the pitch, it is refreshing to see one of the biggest names in the English game keeping his feet firmly on the ground and behaving in the right way. Like many Premier League and England stars, Defoe has had a lot written about him in the national media, and not all of it shows him in a positive light. However, one of the most regular observations by those who have written about him is that he is a regular churchgoer who loves his mother dearly. While he has enjoyed some of the trappings that fame and fortune bring, he has always remained grounded.

In an interview with the *Mirror* in 2006 he said: 'I like to go to church whenever I can. Sometimes we [Spurs] do a warm down on a Sunday so I can't go, but if we have a day off then

I get a phone call from my mum at eight o'clock in the morning. I used to go to church when I was younger so I don't see why I shouldn't go to church now. I think it gives you mental strength, it puts things in perspective, especially when things aren't going so well for you, so it's been good for me. I like to say my prayers and it's something I've always done. My mum enjoys it, my family too.'

Defoe prays before every game without fail and is always sure to give thanks, whether things are going well for him or he is going through a tough time. This follows on from his youth, when Sunday football would be followed by a trip to church with his mother. Prayer and football always did go hand in hand for him. And he is not alone. While footballers are often perceived as fame-hungry millionaires with a penchant for cars, women and big nights out, Defoe has revealed there are other players who follow his lifestyle of church on a Sunday and prayer before every game. In the same *Mirror* interview he told how former Tottenham left-back Lee Young-Pyo also regularly attended church, and how he would often speak to the South Korean international about their religious beliefs when they first became team-mates at White Hart Lane.

So with a healthy sense of faith and belief, a loving family and a true sense of grounding, it was no surprise that Defoe was perfectly equipped to follow his dream in the early stages of his life. Like any other player, his earliest memories of the game came from his schooldays, particularly as a secondary school pupil at St Bonaventure's. As a youth he played for the famous boys' club Senrab before being snapped up by Charlton Athletic, but it was at school that Defoe began to make a name for himself in the game he loved. He often goes back to visit his old school, and the youngsters there today no doubt take inspiration from their local hero. He takes inspiration from them as well.

St Bonaventure's, more commonly known as St Bon's, was and still is one of the most popular schools in east London. Located in Forest Gate, it is known for being heavily oversubscribed (there are three applications for every place in year seven) as local families look for a good education for their sons. Originally a grammar school, it became the first voluntary aided comprehensive school to be awarded technology college status in the area. As a result it has an excellent reputation for developing youngsters, with Ofsted reports praising it for being 'outstandingly effective' and being able to foster exemplary behaviour among its pupils.

St Bon's also prides itself on giving local youngsters the chance to thrive in an active and multicultural setting – more than 70 per cent of its intake are from an Afro-Caribbean background – and enjoys a tremendous reputation in the neighbourhood. According to the school's website, 'St Bonaventure's school is founded on Christian principles and enriched by the cultural and religious diversity of its environment. We endeavour to be a community where each individual can grow spiritually, academically and socially.' The school aims to create a disciplined environment where the Roman Catholic faith is central to each pupil's academic life, while remaining a place that encourages warm and respectful relationships.

The school does not cite sporting achievement as one of its outstanding features, perhaps because the nearest grass football pitches are situated three miles away at Wanstead Flats. It comes as something of a surprise, then, that its list of alumni includes Chris Hughton (former assistant manager of Tottenham during

Defoe's first spell there and then Newcastle boss), former Spurs and Leyton Orient winger John Chiedozie, Nigel Callaghan (who played more than 200 games for Watford), and ex-Leyton Orient player and manager Martin Ling. But perhaps the most famous footballing name to have undertaken his secondary education at St Bon's is Jermain Defoe.

It is fair to say that Defoe's main focus at school was not his education. He wanted to play football. All the time. But that desire to play simply fuelled a desire to get to school so that he *could* play. On a visit to his old stomping ground in 2005 he told the *Evening Standard*: 'I'd get here at 7.30am to play and was worn out before school started. Then it was hard to concentrate on school work; I used to sit in class and dream of the bell so I could go outside and play football.' He was no tearaway at school. He was always there and he always behaved himself. But he just could not resist the chance to kick a ball around with his friends.

There was one fenced-off area of the playground known as 'the cage'. This was where the big lads in year 11 would play. It was not a place for the pint-sized like Defoe, but thanks to his football-playing cousins, he would be allowed to sneak in and give some of the bigger boys a taste of what was to come. What he lacked in physical size he more than made up for in confidence in his own ability and sheer love of the game.

When it came to school football teams, Defoe was not surprisingly something of a talisman. On his return to St Bon's in 2005 he was reminded by a pupil of a primary school game he played in – the pupil's older brother still tells the story of how he managed to tackle Defoe during the match. Perhaps what he mentions less was the 9-2 scoreline, helped by five goals from the developing marksman. Even so, this was not the high point: while representing St Bonaventure's in the Newham and Essex Schools Cup final he walloped six, and that was before half-time.

But the greatest indication of how important this school was in shaping the young Defoe and readying him for the world ahead is the time he gives to and affection he still holds for the place. Defoe was only a student at St Bon's for three years before being snapped up by Charlton Athletic and sent to the Football Association's national academy at Lilleshall, but he still comes back to the school with some regularity. He still feels he owes something to the place because, deep down, he knows his school gave him a great deal. 'When people ask, "How come you're so down to earth?" I say a lot is to do with my school and what I learned there, the discipline, the hard work,' he revealed to the *Evening Standard*.

It might seem an obvious thing to say, but in an age where many young footballers barely attend school, Defoe's healthy relationship with the place that gave him an education is refreshing. The ideas of discipline and hard work are often spoken of by teachers and football managers alike – proof that thriving in one environment is not mutually exclusive from thriving in the other. For the developing Defoe, the preparation he received in his short time at St Bon's was enough to teach him how to carry himself as he embarked on the tricky journey to a professional career in the sport he was desperate to succeed in. It is also why his return to the school is always met with immense pride by those who remember him.

'Mr Skelton could always be a bit scary,' said Defoe of assistant head Brian Skelton when he was back at school to visit in 2005. But there is no doubt in Skelton's mind that his former pupil is one of the most important people in the school's past – and future. He remains impressed by Defoe's desire to come back and see how things are getting on – although he admits it can be a bit of a nightmare at a school filled with football-crazy youngsters. 'The situation could get completely out of control,' Skelton told the *Evening Standard*. 'Still, at least he gives us a bit of notice these days. He used to pop in unannounced and it was absolute bedlam.'

Bedlam it may have been but that did not stop Defoe joining the students in a kickabout when the opportunity presented itself. Playing football at school was what he was used to, and so was playing football against boys bigger than he was. 'I'm still not as big as some of this lot,' he laughed. But in that situation alone, it was clear to see that Jermain Defoe the schoolboy, Jermain Defoe the man and Jermain Defoe the professional football star were truly all one and the same. A genuine sense of fun, a genuine sense of knowing where he came from and a genuine sense of pride in what he does now all show how he can influence those who want to travel down the same path to go about it in the right way.

He added: 'This place is a part of me. It's important to come back here – it reminds me where I'm from. I grew up, a young boy playing football in the streets. Things have happened so quickly for me – playing in the Premiership, playing for England – but it's still the same old me really.' It is a true emotional connection to his past from a man who spent just three years at a place so dear to his heart. There are people who can spend seven years of their life at school and not feel any bond with it in the slightest. Not Jermain Defoe. That is something for which he, and St Bonaventure's, deserves some credit.

But there was a lot more in Defoe's youth that set him on the road to football stardom. It is important to remember his stay at secondary school was not a long one. At just 14 years of age he was snapped up by Charlton Athletic and thrust into the FA National School of Excellence at Lilleshall, where he would be introduced to the professional standards that were to be demanded of him for the rest of his playing career. That move came about as a result of his regular Sunday activities. Not church, but Sunday youth football.

Defoe did not just play for any old weekend boys' club. Senrab FC is based in east London and plays its matches on Wanstead Flats, so it seemed a perfect fit for a local lad who wanted to spend all his free time playing football. It was no surprise that Defoe ended up part of what has become a conveyor belt of talent and one of the most important football clubs in London. It was there that Charlton spotted him and it was in those early days of competitive football that Defoe really learned his footballing trade. It was one thing scoring goals for fun in schoolboy matches, but doing it on a regular basis at a high-profile amateur club standard was something to make the London scouting network sit up and take notice.

Established in 1961, Senrab – named after a road in Stepney – is one of the most renowned youth football clubs in the country. Running teams for children aged between five and 17 years of age, the club allows boys from east London the chance to play football locally to a standard which allows them to flourish under its excellent coaching and in conditions that belie the often complicated social surroundings that the youngsters see on a daily basis. The sort of council estate violence that has become a feature of such areas as Beckton is kept far away by a club that instils a level of sporting discipline in its players while maintaining high levels of enjoyment.

Senrab's club secretary Tony Carroll explained to *BBC Sport* in 2004 exactly what the club was all about. 'All of the staff give their time freely. We get paid by seeing the boys enjoying themselves, improving and if they join a club then you know you've done a good job. Players also have a code of conduct. We've thrown people out of the club for misbehaving, for causing aggravation at games and in training. But if people want their boys to play football, then they come to us.'

Carroll added that the best players technically do not necessarily have what it takes to progress to the next level. 'There are thousands of kids that have got the talent but haven't got the right temperament. You can send a player to a professional club and think he's the best thing since sliced bread but then they send him back two weeks later because his time-keeping is poor and he's not disciplined. The players have to be 100 per cent committed and if they're not then they're wasting the club's time.'

A number of future professionals have donned the black and red stripes of Senrab and some have gone on to play for England (one, former Leicester City man Muzzy Izzet, went on to play for Turkey). Spurs and Arsenal defensive stalwart Sol Campbell, Tottenham skipper Ledley King, West Ham, Spurs and Fulham pair Bobby Zamora and Paul Konchesky, Birmingham midfielder Lee Bowyer, Bolton full-back Jloyd Samuel and Chelsea captain John Terry were all members of east London's most celebrated amateur football set-up. It's not only players who make their name at Senrab. Coaches who have gone on to make their name in the professional arena include former Charlton and West Ham boss Alan Curbishley, Chelsea assistant manager Ray Wilkins, Crewe Alexandra and youth talent-spotting legend Dario Gradi, and West Ham United's director of youth development Tony Carr. No doubt then, that Senrab was the best place to be for a young footballer in east London.

Such is the reputation of Senrab that its reach has spread beyond its local base in the East End of London. Now players come from Essex to test themselves at a club that is known as the finest in town for bringing the best out of its young footballers. It is no small feat that the club has managed to cultivate such a fantastic standing, despite not owning its own facilities for playing or even training: Wanstead Flats are council pitches that are used by amateur footballers from leagues all over London and Essex.

There is certainly no other club like Senrab in London, perhaps in the country, and its members develop strong bonds. Another Senrab old boy is the much-travelled striker Ade Akinbiyi. He recalls his time at Senrab fondly and the great friendship with Sol Campbell he developed there. 'I have known him since we used to play against each other in Sunday football when we were about 13,' Akinbiyi told *This is London* in 2002. 'I played for Senrab and he ended up joining us on a tour to Ayr in Scotland. Our friendship started from there. We didn't live too far apart: he was in Stratford and I was just down the road in Hackney. I used to see him a lot and we went out together until he went up to Lilleshall.' Both players have been through difficult periods in their career since those days, but Akinbiyi says his friendship with Campbell has remained strong and the two have helped each other through the tough times.

Jermain Defoe was a Senrab player some years after those two, but he made some solid friendships of his own. One of them was with a young man named Leon Knight, who would also go into the game. Knight signed for Chelsea as a trainee before having spells at Brighton & Hove Albion, Swansea City, Milton Keynes Dons and Wycombe Wanderers, among other clubs. At Senrab, they seemed like two peas in a pod. Both were small. Both were quick. Both were strikers. But perhaps the most important characteristic that drew them together was a love of scoring goals.

In a 2005 interview with the *Evening Standard*, Knight recalled how the two of them had met. 'At Senrab, the coach put us into groups to practise our passing. I was with Jermain and we just clicked,' said Knight. 'He would come round to my house to watch football videos. Football was our interest at that age: we would study the techniques of Pelé or Maradona. Ian Wright was another hero and we even tried to emulate his goal celebrations. I think Jermain still does. We scored countless goals for Senrab – we connected really well as a partnership. We were Dwight Yorke and Andy Cole before they even happened.'

The two young forwards became something of a double-act as their time at Senrab continued. Their coaches could not help but be impressed. Here were two boys, both in love with football, and both having the time of their lives with every passing game. What more could a youth coach want? Carroll still recalls how well they performed on the pitch. While Knight was with Swansea in 2006, Carroll spoke to *Wales on Sunday* and explained what it was like to have two such goal-hungry teens in his side. He said: 'They were absolutely unbelievable as a partnership – just like a pair of whippets, so very, very quick. You could see they had a bit of class, even at 13 or 14 years of age. They just used to dish out the goals between them. The team would win 6-0 and they would score three each. There was always a bit of friendly rivalry to see who could score the most.'

Another of Defoe's coaches at Senrab, Billy Boorman, also remembers Defoe and Knight running riot throughout their early teens. In fact, Boorman saw the two of them grow up together, having coached their year group from under-10 to under-14 level. He told the *Evening Standard* in 2004: 'The pair of them used to wear yellow Brazil shirts and then go out and play like Brazilians. I've known Jermain since he was nine. He was a lovely kid, always really attentive. He had a great attitude and really wanted to achieve.' Boorman did have one surprise, however. 'He was a provider as much as a goalscorer,' he revealed. 'I used to play him in midfield when he was younger.' Surely not! 'But later I pushed him forward with Leon.' How different Defoe's career might have been, had he stayed in midfield!

Defoe's Senrab career earned him a reputation at the club. His coaches knew him as a precocious talent with an eye for goal, and his fellow players knew him as a football-loving workaholic – always honing his technique and making sure he knew exactly what he had to do put the ball in the back of the net. Defoe and Knight would pick up a great deal from watching Pelé and Maradona on video, but the one name that stands out in Knight's list of boyhood idols is that of Arsenal legend Ian Wright. How ironic that the man who was once the Gunners' record goalscorer would be the hero of a youngster who would go on to be idolised in the same way at bitter rivals Tottenham. 'I loved him,' Defoe admitted in 2004. 'He was a legend. I used to say to all my friends that I'd just love to meet him. All his experiences, all those goals.'

Indeed it was 'all those goals' that drew early comparisons between Defoe and Wright from another of Senrab's coaches. Paul Rolls was a coach at the club before taking scouting roles at Charlton and West Ham, and eventually becoming involved in taking Defoe to Upton Park. In a 2004 interview with the *Evening Standard* he said, 'Jermain once told me he modelled himself on Ian Wright. Look at the way he plays now – it is almost identical to Wright.' But Rolls made another was one further comment that cannot go unnoticed: 'Jermain was an Arsenal fanatic – he used to hate Spurs.' One gets the feeling that the 'hatred' has subsided somewhat with time!

It was not only team-mates, coaches and opponents of Senrab who knew all about Defoe. The boy was making a name for himself with some of the older lads at the club as well. Shortly before Spurs played Chelsea in 2004, and shortly after Defoe had scored his first England goal, his schoolboy days were remembered by someone a little bit older from the same background – Chelsea captain John Terry. He recounted to the *Sunday Mirror* in 2004: 'Jermain is as sharp as anything. When we played as kids we [the older boys] used to come off the pitch having won our game four or five-nil and would be happy with ourselves. The team a year younger than us would be on the next pitch, so we'd ask how they'd done. Jermain would just say "Oh, I scored six today." That was a regular occurrence.'

Despite difficult circumstances in his earliest years, Defoe's love of football appeared to have put him on the right track to success. Backed by the love and support of his mother and grandmother, he was able to focus all his attention on the game he was desperate to succeed in. The more he saw of his heroes the more he wanted to be like them. The more he wanted to be like them the more he would practise. And the more he practised the better he became. Better ball control. Better dribbling ability. Better at putting the ball in the back of the net. And with more goals came more recognition.

Senrab knew that the very best players who came through their ranks would be given serious consideration by the professional clubs nearby. For Defoe to step up to the next level he needed to make sure that London's football elite knew who he was. Two clubs linked closely to Senrab were West Ham United and Charlton Athletic. A number of the Sunday league outfit's coaches were involved in scouting and coaching young local talent there, and with so many goals to his name, it came as little surprise that the diminutive Defoe was at the top of their wish list. It was Charlton who encouraged the youngster to join them, but only after he had been through the rigours of Lilleshall.

Defoe was 14 when he attended trials at the Football Association's national academy in 1997 – 'I really wanted to go and realised it was such a great opportunity,' he told the *Independent* in 2004. A great opportunity indeed at a time when progression through the FA's School of Excellence was still a potential fast-track into the professional game. Sunday League football with Senrab was one thing, being on Charlton's books quite another. Lilleshall was quite simply the peak of youth football in the country. Once you had made it through there, you were good enough to start thinking about a career in the game. That was what was expected of those who made it through.

Although Lilleshall no longer exists as a national football

academy, it is still seen as something of a benchmark for players of a certain generation. The Shropshire base ended its association with the FA in 1999 but its football training and education methods were adopted by the individual club academies that took its place. But between 1984 and 1999 there was no better place in the country for a young footballer to really learn his trade. The list of Lilleshall students to have made it to the top of the English game makes impressive reading. As well as Senrab old boy Sol Campbell, future England star Michael Owen, and Liverpool and England defender Jamie Carragher (a Champions League winner) are both graduates of the School of Excellence, as are Premier League regulars and England internationals Joe Cole, Wes Brown and Scott Parker.

In the initial trials Defoe attended there were two thousand boys all hoping to earn a place at the academy. He knew it would take something special to separate himself from all the other young hopefuls and gain the opportunity of a lifetime. For him, there was only one way to do that, and that was to do what he did best: score goals. After successfully negotiating the early stages, he made it to the final 16 players in a two-day trial at Lilleshall itself. Again, he knew that goals would have to be the answer if he was to show what he was made of in just two matches. In the first game he scored five goals, and by the time the second match came round, it was clear that no other boy could match his effort. As if to the hammer the point home, Defoe laced up his shooting boots again and put away five more.

It would have been easy for Defoe to step off the pitch and feel certain that he had made it through the trials. Scoring ten goals in two games is a remarkable feat, a wonderful achievement at any level. But the teenager was not convinced. He knew he had done well on the pitch but when the letter came through his door to reveal his footballing fate he was far too nervous to open it. Once again, it was up to Mum to help him through – 'You're in!'

From there it seemed as though Defoe's career would take the path mapped out for him by those at the Valley. Having made it to the national academy, he went on to graduate successfully and joined up with Charlton's youth team. Two successful years under the watchful eye of first-team manager Alan Curbishley suggested that the boy from Beckton would go on to sign professional terms with the Addicks and help them preserve their newfound Premier League status. However, Defoe was about to make a decision that would change his football career – and his life.

Chapter 2
The Pro

In 1999, just before his 17th birthday, Defoe signed professional terms with West Ham. In the eyes of those at Charlton who had helped him with his football education it was seen as a dramatic and unwelcome u-turn. A Football Association tribunal ruled that West Ham would have to pay Charlton in the region of £1.5 million in compensation, plus 15 per cent of any transfer fees received for him. In the eyes of Addicks manager Alan Curbishley and the Valley faithful this was nowhere near enough for such a talented prospect, to whom Charlton had given a first opportunity with a professional club and much of the basis for a football career.

Defoe insists he chose West Ham to further his career, and looking back that move seems justified. It gained him regular Premier League football and a place in the national team, but Curbishley remained angry with the way he felt Charlton were treated. He said: 'The Defoe transfer still rankles here. We wanted the right money and £1.5 million isn't adequate for a Premier League player. We wanted the right money, which we didn't get, and we wanted a situation which forced other clubs to think twice about the risk of going to a tribunal.' As for the Charlton fans, they have made no secret of their feelings towards Defoe, regarding him as having walked out on the club after all it had done for him, despite having never played a first-team game. They have let him know just how they feel in every return he has made to the Valley since. That started with a reserve game for the Hammers shortly after the move. 'I hadn't been to the Valley for ages but the stick I got was unbelievable,' Defoe recalled.

But when all was said and done the journey north of the Thames looked like being the perfect move for the developing striker. After all, Upton Park was not nicknamed 'The Academy' of football for nothing. The club's history of producing and nurturing young, talented players and turning them into stars is famous in English football. World Cup winners Sir Geoff Hurst, Martin Peters and the late Bobby Moore all came through the club's youth ranks as boys, as did Sir Trevor Brooking, Harry Redknapp (then the Hammers manager) and Defoe's former boss Curbishley. When Defoe joined on the cusp of the millennium he could look to the likes of Rio Ferdinand, Joe Cole, Michael Carrick and Frank Lampard (following in the footsteps of his father, Frank senior) for inspiration to reach the first team.

It certainly seemed as though he was inspired. Defoe hit the ground running at his new club, his goals helping fire the under-19 team to the Premiership Academy title in the 1999/2000 season, including a double against the club he had supported as a boy, Arsenal, in the play-off final. A first-team call-up was inevitable for a player whose only aim on the pitch was to score goals. Nothing else would do. Redknapp was impressed right away. 'When we got him from Charlton he was banging them in for the youth team, then the reserves, right up to the first team,' he recalled in 2004. 'Right from the off Jermain was a hit. He was so full of confidence and the self-belief of youth that he didn't need time to settle in. Show him a goal and he's away, like a wind-up toy.'

If Defoe needed any more inspiration, it would come in the form of a childhood idol. When Defoe joined West Ham, Ian Wright had just finished his long spell at Arsenal and had joined the Hammers as his glittering career began to come to an end. Finally, Defoe could realise his dream of meeting the man he had dreamed of emulating. Finally, he could learn from the man he saw as a true master of scoring goals. Despite being more than twice Defoe's age (36 to his 17), Wright would stay behind after training at the club's Chadwell Heath training ground and give the teenage starlet the benefit of his years of experience at the highest level.

'Training with him, for me, was unbelievable,' Defoe said. 'As I was running into the box he would hold me – literally hold me back by the shirt – and then, when it was time, he would say, "Right – go now!"' Defoe is proud to say the two of them have stayed close as his career has developed, with Wright acting as something of a mentor to the man seen by many as a modern version of the Gunners great.

Under the tutelage of his football hero and the guidance of a West Ham legend at a club where young players were not only taught how to play at the top level but also given the chance to do so, Defoe could hardly have been better placed to take his career to the next step as a new professional. It is true that his move from Charlton caused something of a stir and left a bitter taste in some mouths, and it would not be the last time in his career that he courted controversy. But the fact remained that the 17-year-old had joined this club to make an impact and to play first team football. After succeeding with the youth team in his first season, Defoe would get his wish the following year.

The 2000/01 season got off to a difficult start for Redknapp's side. An opening day 4-2 defeat at London rivals Chelsea was followed by a disappointing 1-0 home reverse against Leicester City. A creditable 2-2 draw with champions Manchester United at Upton Park showed signs of improvement as did another share of the spoils with Sunderland at the Stadium of Light. However, another defeat in another London derby, 1-0 at the hands of Spurs at White Hart Lane, meant the Hammers had not managed a win in their opening six games as they headed into the first leg of a League Cup second round tie against Walsall on Tuesday 19 September.

A rainy night at the Bescot Stadium is perhaps not the ideal setting for the start of a football fairytale. But as those that follow the game know so well, the greatest of stories can take place in the most unexpected of situations. The change in fortunes that West Ham were seeking did not necessarily bring about a change in the starting line-up. The fact was that they saw the chance to progress in the first cup competition of the season against Division Two opposition as the perfect opportunity to get that first win in a troublesome start to the campaign. As a result, Defoe was on the bench. Redknapp knew his young starlet was not yet ready for a starting berth. But he also knew that if he needed a goal, he had just the lad to come off the bench and get one.

It was a tough game for the visitors, as is always the case when a top-flight team travels to play on lower-league soil, but they looked to impose themselves on their less illustrious opposition early on. Former academy player Joe Cole was looking nimble and lively, serving to show the watching Defoe what was possible if you put in the work and expressed your ability as a West Ham teenager. It was Cole's sharpness of mind that almost helped give his side the lead on the night, with a searching long ball that found former QPR winger and future England international Trevor Sinclair on the right wing, but his pullback to Northern Ireland midfielder Steve Lomas was blocked by the Walsall defence. Sinclair himself had the first real chance of the game as he latched on to a through ball from England legend Stuart Pearce but his low effort produced a stunning save from James Walker, a man who would go on to play for the Hammers later in his career.

The likes of Sinclair, Lomas and Pearce, along with former Arsenal full-back Nigel Winterburn, Croatian defender Igor Stimac and West Ham regular Steve Potts, complemented the youthful exuberance of players like Cole, Rio Ferdinand and Michael Carrick. It was proof that Defoe was in the perfect place to continue his football development. The blend of guile and experience, coupled with expressiveness and fearlessness, showed that two different generations of the game could co-exist with remarkable efficiency and offer the perfect learning experience for any young professional.

As the first half wore on it looked like it was going to be a frustrating night for the Hammers. Cole was involved again with an industrious run down the right wing before crossing for Winterburn to head home, but the side's senior player had his effort ruled out for handball. When the second half came, though briefly interrupted by the surprise of a male streaker, Walsall looked determined to capitalise on the Londoners' profligacy in front of goal. Portuguese striker Jorge Leitão and winger Darren Byfield were denied clear runs on goal by the excellent defending of Ferdinand and Stimac respectively, before Pedro Matias was put clean through by Gabor Bukran, only for Potts to save the day with a wonderful last-ditch challenge. On 67 minutes Leitão was first to reach a hopeful long ball from Matias but was denied by the sharp thinking of Shaka Hislop in goal.

The West Ham manager had seen enough. His team was looking vulnerable at the back, but crucially there was little left to offer up front. Redknapp knew it was time to change things. It was time to unleash his soon-to-be not-so-secret weapon. With 77 minutes on the clock, Jermain Defoe was given his first-team debut with one simple task: find a winning goal. And as in so many of the games he played growing up – at school, at Senrab, at Lilleshall, in academy football – the boy wonder did not have to wait long.

West Ham began to press forward and with just six minutes left, forced a corner when Pearce's attempted cross was blocked. Carrick trotted over to take the kick, knowing the delivery had to be good to create the chance that the Londoners desperately needed. The young Geordie's cross caused mayhem in the Saddlers' penalty area and the ball broke to Ferdinand. His shot rattled the crossbar from close range and fell invitingly eight yards from goal. It just needed someone in the right place at the right time to finish the job. With an instinctive reaction, Defoe pounced on the loose ball and made no mistake with a finish so cool and collected one could be forgiven for thinking he had been playing up front for years. Not so. He was still a month shy of his 18th birthday and this was the first time he had played a first-team game. Jermain Defoe had arrived.

Having grabbed the goal, West Ham clung on to win the game. There was still a second leg at Upton Park to come but they had overcome a massive psychological hurdle by finally winning their first game of the season. And they had done it thanks to a striker who was unknown to the wider football audience. However, Defoe would not be around to help West Ham in the second leg. His astute manager had realised that if the club's newest hero was going to make real progress, he would need regular first-team football. The problem was that the West Ham squad already contained superstar Paolo Di Canio, new signing Frederic Kanoute and Croatian hero Davor Suker, so first-team opportunities would be strictly limited. It is hard enough to keep big name players happy when they are not playing, let alone when their place in the team is being taken by an unknown teenager.

The solution was to send Defoe away on loan. A full season under his belt, albeit further down the Football League ladder, would give the youngster a chance to continue his development along the right lines. Playing further down the leagues would not bother Defoe in the slightest. A goal is a goal wherever you score it, was the attitude he clearly held throughout his formative years. But where to send him? It needed to be a club that Redknapp knew well and trusted to do right by his young forward. The answer was AFC Bournemouth.

Redknapp had been the most successful manager in Bournemouth's history, taking them to the second tier of English football for the first time after winning the Third Division in 1987. He had also achieved fame on the south coast by masterminding a famous FA Cup third-round shock victory over Manchester United in 1984. In addition, he had given his son Jamie his professional debut there as a 16-year-old. Now in Division Two and managed by fledgling boss Sean O'Driscoll, who liked to get the ball down and play, the Dean Court club was the perfect place to send West Ham's latest golden boy to ready himself for the Premier League.

Defoe joined Bournemouth with healthy reputation and O'Driscoll was willing to give him the opportunity to play from the start as soon as he arrived. That said, it may not have been the hardest decision the young manager had ever had to make. Bournemouth's season had not got off to the best of starts. They had mustered only two wins in their opening 15 games, a 3-0 win at home to Swindon and a 5-2 win at Gigg Lane against Bury. In short, they were struggling and looked like early-season candidates for a relegation scrap. It was a lot to ask of a teenager to keep them in the division on his own.

Bournemouth's next match took them up north to Stoke for a game in which Defoe would make his full first-team debut. With so little going right on the pitch for the Cherries, O'Driscoll knew the time was right to make a major change to his team. In adding a youngster with an eye for goal to the mix, he also knew he had a quick and nimble forward that the opposition would know nothing about. If his new signing could flourish, they would have a great chance of picking up three valuable points to put their season back on track. He got half of what he was after.

Bournemouth's disappointing start to the season had left the players low on confidence. That much was evident in the opening stages of the game as Stoke raced into a two-goal lead after just 13 minutes. Bournemouth were lacking any real imagination until the new boy suddenly clicked into gear. He began to torment the Stoke defenders with his pace and trickery, rattling the woodwork twice in quick succession, first by thumping a shot against the bar and then driving onto the post. It seemed only a matter of time before the inevitable happened and sure enough he pulled his side back into the game with a bullet header from close range. He had scored two debut goals within six weeks of each other.

Unfortunately for Bournemouth they could not use Defoe's moment of inspiration as a platform to turn the game around, despite Stoke's manager Gudjon Thordarson being sent to the stands for a confrontation with the fourth official. The Cherries' Richard Hughes also saw a second-half penalty saved by Potters keeper Carl Muggleton as the visitors were unable to capitalise on their momentum. They had lost again, but O'Driscoll knew that with better luck they would have come away with more. 'Jermain gave us another dimension and, with a bit more luck, he could have scored four,' the manager commented afterwards.

It was clear to O'Driscoll that Defoe would be a crucial part of their immediate future. If Bournemouth were going to force their way up the league, they needed Defoe to show the sort of form his debut had promised. For a teenager just taking his first steps in the professional game, that gave him all the confidence he needed. He had a manager at his host club ready to give him all the games he needed to show what he could do, and another at his parent club who had a place waiting for him if he came back to London having impressed. It was simple enough: keep scoring goals and keep moving forward.

Bournemouth's performance at Stoke had been an improvement but the fact remained that they needed to stop

the rot. Their next game was against Peterborough at home –
the perfect opportunity to build on the progress they had
made at the Britannia Stadium. Again O'Driscoll trusted
Defoe with a place in the starting eleven, and again he would
provide evidence that there were big things to come. It took
the 18-year-old just 20 minutes to make himself known to the
Bournemouth faithful on the first of many appearances at
Dean Court.

Despite having lost their last two matches the home side
looked rejuvenated. They were playing with renewed vigour
and now possessed a genuine threat up front, with Defoe's
ability causing no end of problems for the Peterborough
defenders. It came as little surprise therefore when he gave his
team the lead. Stephen Purches sent over an excellent cross
which left Defoe the easiest of chances to nod home from close
range. He was barely over five and a half feet tall and not yet
fully developed physically, but already he had managed to
score two headers in two games. The rough and tumble nature
of the Football League certainly did not seem to faze the new
darling of Dean Court.

The young loanee continued to torment the Posh back line
and probably should have doubled his tally when he found
himself clean through on goal. However, in a rare lapse of
concentration he failed to control the ball and the chance was
gone. Perhaps it was a good thing to get the technical mistakes
out of the way early in his career; at 18 years of age there is
no shame in not getting everything right first time. 'I am still
learning – that is why I am here,' he said after the match.

The Cherries took their one-goal lead into half-time, but
they made things hard for themselves just 30 seconds into the
second period. Carl Fletcher was given his marching orders

after picking up his second yellow card and all of a sudden the hosts were facing an uphill battle. The momentum was with the away side and they made their numerical advantage count when Dave Farrell grabbed an equaliser. It looked as though it was going to be a third straight game without a win for Bournemouth – until they got the lucky break their early endeavours deserved, a late free-kick from Wayne Cummings deflecting into the back of the net. That made it three wins in total for the season, but with a new striker scoring goals, the feeling was growing that the team would not be languishing at the bottom of the table for very long. If they continued in the same vein, playing the same kind of football and building the team around the irrepressible Defoe, a climb up the league was certainly on the cards.

With form returning fast to Bournemouth, it seemed like the perfect time to play Northampton Town at Sixfields. A growing injury list had left the Cobblers down to the bare bones in a very busy period of games, and a visit from a side who looked like they were about to hit their stride was the last thing they wanted. It showed on the pitch as a Defoe-inspired performance inflicted their heaviest defeat of the season.

It took a while for the visitors to go in front but Steve Fletcher's 25-yard free-kick on 37 minutes was worth the wait. With the lead established and the nerves settled, Bournemouth took the game by the scruff of the neck and the crowd were treated to an early edition of the Jermain Defoe show. The talented teenager doubled the visiting side's advantage on the hour mark with a goal at the second attempt after his first effort had been blocked by the Northampton defence. There was more to come as a shot of genuine power flew beyond Northampton keeper Keith Welch and into the net via the post. That made it four goals in three games for his new club, and five goals in just four first-team appearances since starting his professional career.

Welch made sure the teenager did not manage his first professional hat-trick with a string of fine saves in the second half, but Northampton had nothing to offer up front as Bournemouth strung back-to-back wins together for the first time that season. After the game O'Driscoll admitted he had taken something of a risk when he decided to sign Defoe, but it looked to be paying off early on as his struggling team were starting to turn the form book on its head. 'Jermain is only 18 and we've taken a bit of a gamble on him,' he revealed. 'But he gives us a threat up front. In our position we have to play youngsters and take a chance.' It was the clearest indication yet from the manager that he intended to use Defoe as much as possible. He believed that West Ham's newest gem (or 'Jem', as he was known at Senrab) would prove to be the catalyst for a successful second half of the season.

Defoe was back on the scoresheet in the next league game. More significantly Bournemouth's 3-0 victory on a trip to Wycombe at the start of December made it three wins in their last four games on the road. It took some more goalkeeping heroics, this time from Martin Taylor, to keep Defoe and Bournemouth from running riot, but it was to little avail as he was left with no chance by three goals of real quality.

First, Jason Tindall found space to cross for Carl Fletcher who swept home with aplomb. Fletcher grabbed a second late on to make it three with a superb strike but it was Defoe's strike, sandwiched between the other two, that was the pick of the bunch by a considerable distance. It was a goal that exemplified all the qualities that he was becoming known for:

pace, quick feet, a devastating shot and an eye for goal. He picked up the ball and began a mazy dribble, taking the ball past three Wycombe defenders before launching an unstoppable rising drive into the far corner to stun the Adams Park crowd and send the pocket of travelling fans into raptures.

By the end then Chairboys manager Lawrie Sanchez had to admit that Bournemouth had dominated the game, conceding they were 'the better team by a mile'. Defoe was quite simply in the form of his young life. He had scored five times since joining Bournemouth on loan and his presence at the club was one of the key reasons for their rapid rise up the table. Thanks to his goals and their improving results, they were going from relegation candidates to play-off contenders. Despite not getting many points on the board early on, they were living proof that a quick run of wins in the league can turn a season on its head. Another win and another starring role from Defoe were on the way, although this time, he was as much the villain as he was the hero.

When Swansea travelled down to Dean Court they were in the middle of a dire run of form. No wins in ten games and nine straight defeats had left them in an unenviable position at the wrong end of the table. While Bournemouth were winning games for fun, Swansea seemed unable to muster a win for love nor money. Bournemouth had already beaten Swansea at home with a 2-0 victory in the FA Cup, and they would be celebrating another win by the same scoreline, with Defoe playing a significant part in both goals. He would also encounter the first major on-field controversy of his fledgling career.

With just half an hour gone Defoe went down in the box under a challenge from Swans keeper Roger Freestone. Referee Lee Cable pointed to the spot but Swansea's players were absolutely convinced that Defoe had dived and, led by Freestone, they let the referee know what they felt. However, the decision stood and Richard Hughes stepped up to slot the penalty calmly beyond the infuriated Freestone and give his side the lead. Swansea manager John Hollins confirmed the stance of his players after the game, joining in the accusations that Defoe had gone down too easily. 'Roger said he touched it and the guy did dive late,' fumed Hollins, adding: 'The boys are furious because they clearly felt it was not a penalty.' He went on to claim that Defoe had dived again later on in the game and complained about him not receiving a booking.

However, Defoe did not let the incident affect his performance – much to the frustration of the beleaguered Swans. Instead he took things in his stride and continued to focus on playing football. It was an approach that paid off shortly after half-time. Jamie Day delivered a long ball over the top that left Defoe one on one with Jason Smith. Instead of attempting to beat his man as he had done in the Wycombe game, he decided to go for goal straight away and unleashed a sumptuous lob from 30 yards that left Freestone completely flat-footed in disbelief. It was certainly not the goalkeeper's day.

Unfortunately, the game took a more bad-tempered turn after Defoe had sealed the win and the teenager became the target of Swansea's frustrations. The Welsh team were convinced that their imminent defeat was the result of his having cheated and he had to deal with some robust challenges in the latter stages. A number of Swansea players found themselves in the referee's notebook and O'Driscoll was forced into substituting Defoe to prevent any nasty consequences. 'Swansea got a bit frustrated with him and I had to take him off for his own protection,' he confirmed at the end.

Even with Defoe no longer on the pitch the game retained an unsavoury element as it entered its closing stages. Swansea substitute Martin Thomas was involved in an ugly clash with striker Steve Fletcher before Swans defender Kristian O'Leary was forced to leave the field with a head injury which required stitches. As if that were not enough, Bournemouth goalkeeper Gareth Stewart was clattered by Steve Watkin and left with stud marks visible down his neck. This was not one for the purists, but the home side had taken all three points and Defoe had been given a taste of just how intense the professional game could become. Whether or not he had been the cause of the ill-feeling on the pitch, he had maintained a high level of performance and managed to keep his head while others around him were losing theirs. This was exemplified by his wonderful goal, proving that both his football sense and common sense were working in tandem.

Defoe's tally now stretched to seven goals in six league games. In terms of making an impact there was little more he could have done. Harry Redknapp had sent him out on loan to get experience of first-team football but not even he could have envisaged that the 18-year-old would go on to take his new club, and Division Two, by storm in such a way. He had scored a marvellous variety of goals already – tap-ins, headers, solo goals and more – and he had not even played ten games as a professional. Bournemouth's fans were starting to get excited as the play-offs became a realistic possibility, but the West Ham fans who were keeping an eye on their future could not help but notice Defoe was getting more prepared for top-flight football with every game he played.

But before any of that he had a goalscoring run to continue. After seven wins in all competitions, Bournemouth were confident heading into their next league fixture, at home against Millwall. For Defoe it was his first opportunity to take on a side from London in a competitive professional fixture. For the first time in seven games the hosts would not have it all their own way and eventually succumbed to a 2-1 defeat. But once again Defoe got himself on the scoresheet to continue his astonishing personal run.

The Lions had taken the lead five minutes before the interval when Christopher Kinet finished off Matt Lawrence's far-post cross before Defoe made every effort to steal the show ten minutes into the second half. Steve Fletcher, who was playing despite the news that his wife had gone into labour hours before kick-off, flicked the ball on towards Defoe, who brought the ball under control and smashed a low drive into the bottom corner with his left foot – another variation on how to score a goal.

Unfortunately for him it was another in-form Division Two striker who stole the headlines as Neil Harris raced on to a headed flick from Paul Moody to fire home his 15th goal of the season to seal all three points for the south Londoners. On the day it was Harris and Millwall who took the plaudits but once again the boy from Beckton was making sure he would not go unnoticed. He simply could not stop scoring. With goals in seven consecutive league games, he was edging ever closer to the record books – and this was still only his first season as a professional. Surely this run could not continue?

Bournemouth's next opponents were Division Two's bottom club Oxford United at the Manor Ground on Boxing Day. Perhaps the run really could continue. And continue it did in truly stylish fashion. Defoe scored twice that day, and so breathtaking was his second goal, the winner in a 2-1 victory, that the *Sun* referred to him as a 'wonder kid'. His performance and all-round contribution suggested that description was not far wide of the mark. Bournemouth were back to winning ways and they had managed it straight after their previous run had come to an end. It looked as though losing to Millwall was only a blip for the Cherries compared to their early season travails.

Defoe had scored the opener after seven minutes, only to see his strike cancelled out by former Wimbledon midfielder Peter Fear moments later. But midway through the second half Defoe restored his side's lead with what manager Sean O'Driscoll referred to as 'one of the best goals you'll see anywhere'. Having picked up the ball around the halfway line Defoe set off on a mesmerising run that carried him fully 40 yards, leaving three Oxford defenders trailing in his wake before he delivered an incredible chip over keeper Neil Cutler from the edge of the box. It was a goal fashioned by industry, craft and vision, and could only have been performed by a player not only of wonderful individual ability, but one who was playing with so much confidence that he believed he could do anything on a football pitch, no matter how difficult.

All that self-belief and confidence in his own ability were brought to the forefront in Bournemouth's next game, a home fixture against Luton on New Year's Day, which turned out to be a genuine thriller. While Bournemouth had pulled themselves clear of the relegation battle and into play-off contention, Luton had struggled for form and found themselves right in the middle of the relegation scrap. It was little surprise when the Cherries took the lead late on in the first period thanks to Fletcher's header.

But Luton clearly had not read the script and two goals in double quick time from Andrew Fotiadis and Adam Locke gave the Hatters a shock lead and silenced the home crowd. Bournemouth huffed and puffed throughout the second half but could not manage to blow Luton's door down, no matter how hard they tried. However, with eight minutes to go they were handed a lifeline when substitute Jude Sterling handled inside the penalty area. Richard Hughes duly obliged from the spot and it looked as though this epic encounter would end in a share of the spoils.

Jermain Defoe was not having that. Jermain Defoe was a winner. If there was a chance to be had in the minutes that remained then there was no doubt in his mind that he would be on the end of it. He had done too much in the previous seven games to let this one fall by the wayside. With five minutes left Bournemouth won a corner and Claus Jorgensen whipped the ball into the danger area. It looked like Luton keeper Mark Ovendale would gather safely but he contrived to drop the ball at the feet of the one player he would be praying to avoid. Eight matches in a row with his name on the scorer's list, and another win for AFC Bournemouth: Defoe was in dreamland. 'We are good enough to reach the playoffs,' he proclaimed after the final whistle, 'and we have a great spirit.'

Defoe was loving every minute of this unbelievable spell. He was now two games away from a record-equalling run of scoring in ten successive league matches. The excitement at Bournemouth was there for all to see. But before any of that he and his team had an important job to do in an FA Cup third round tie, at home to Gillingham. A bad decision from the officials left the hosts feeling a sense of injustice as they succumbed to a 3-2 defeat, but Defoe made sure he grabbed another goal for himself.

Chris Hope had given the visitors an early lead but once again the star of the show took it upon himself to haul his team back into the game immediately with an excellent finish from Steve Fletcher's pass. The partnership between Defoe and Fletcher was proving to be a fruitful one and Fletcher himself had to score a second equaliser after Gills' player-manager Andy Hessenthaler had restored his side's lead.

Then came the controversy as Paul Shaw raced through to score what turned out to be the winning goal. However, video evidence proved that he was yards offside and there was no way the goal should have stood. It cost Bournemouth a place in the next round and denied Defoe the opportunity to showcase himself against bigger and better opposition. If he was going to play against the best, he was going to have to keep on scoring and earn a place in West Ham's first team next season.

Back in Division Two, the perfect ten was drawing nearer. First Defoe had to go through league game number nine, against Wrexham at the Racecourse Ground. Again he did not have to wait long to open the scoring. After six minutes he beat the offside trap and slotted home the 12th goal of his professional career in his 11th professional start. James Hayter doubled Bournemouth's advantage but goals from Kevin Russell and Mark McGregor right at the death prevented the Cherries from picking up their fourth victory in a row on their travels. After the game Wrexham manager Brian Flynn was quick to praise the teenager. 'We knew he'd be a handful,' he said. 'After his experience scoring goals in a lower division, he will be worth more money when he goes back to West Ham.'

Defoe's tenth league game would be against Cambridge United at the Abbey Stadium. If he could score here it would be ten league games in a row – an achievement only matched in the modern era by Liverpool legend John Aldridge, and surpassed only by Dixie Dean for Everton in the 1930s. The only player to have topped that was Pelé, who managed to score in 14 games in a row while playing for Santos. One more goal would put Defoe in excellent company.

Despite Bournemouth going down to ten men after Wade Elliott was sent off, and abysmal weather making the playing conditions tough for all involved, Defoe would not be denied. With 64 minutes on the clock, Fletchers Steve and Carl combined to find the teenager, who slipped his marker and rounded the goalkeeper before slotting the ball home for his 12th league goal in ten league games. He had done it! A record-breaker at 18 years of age with only 12 professional matches to his name, Jermain Defoe had proved he was here to stay. And with Harry Redknapp's number two Frank Lampard senior watching from the stands, word of his achievement would quickly get back to Upton Park.

Redknapp was certainly proud of his young striking sensation. 'He's done great,' he said. 'I sent him out to Bournemouth to get some experience playing league football and he's coped marvellously. To score ten goals in ten games is a terrific achievement. He's a bright lad who's full of confidence. Nothing knocks him – he's a typical goal-scorer. If he misses, he'll be there the next time looking for a goal. He's a kid with a big future. Hopefully, he'll come back to West Ham and establish himself in our first team.'

Defoe himself claimed the Dixie Dean record was not something he was concerned with. He just wanted to continue to do well at Bournemouth and develop as a young footballer. That was music to O'Driscoll's ears, and further evidence that Defoe's attitude was just about perfect for a young footballer with the world at his feet. 'I think Jermain appreciates that you don't win records in football playing on your own,' the Bournemouth manager added, 'so it was a team effort and the boys have had to work hard. He's a young lad who's come into a young side and they've done their bit to improve him as a player.'

Defoe loved Bournemouth and Bournemouth loved Defoe. It was looking like a match made in heaven, for the time being at least. But all good things must come to an end. As much as Defoe was looking like eclipsing Dixie Dean's seven-decade record, and as astonishing as it would have been for the rookie to beat the great Pelé's all-time record, his next game would prove to be the end of this incredible chapter in his football career. It spoke volumes that much of the coverage of Bournemouth's 1-0 victory at Millwall centred on the fact that Defoe had not managed to score. The *Daily Star*'s match report even led on the teenager failing to improve on his impressive record, rather than Claus Jorgensen's early winner.

It seemed a shame that the run came to a halt in his first outing to London in a first-team fixture, but far more important was Bournemouth's impressive away win against the promotion chasing Lions to enhance their own play-off hopes. Manager O'Driscoll took the sensible view, saying that it was far more important for his temporary leader of the line to concentrate on contributing to the team in other ways, not just with his goals. 'I'm glad the run is over because now he can get back to playing,' he said. 'Before the game, Jermain would have settled for the three points and not scoring.'

So there was more evidence that Defoe was displaying an excellent attitude. Many young players get carried away all too easily when things go well for them, but it seemed Defoe knew that hard work and application was the way for him to keep moving forward. The only reason he could keep scoring goals was because he was continuing to put the work in for the team. He had developed a sense of professional pride – despite having only been a professional for little over a year – that meant he was more worried about Bournemouth's league position that any individual accolades. Of course he wanted to play well, but he wanted to play well in a team that was winning.

Unfortunately but not unexpectedly given his age, the regularity with which Defoe was finding the back of the net now began to dwindle. And as Defoe scored fewer goals, the team picked up fewer points. Following the win at the New Den, Bournemouth went the next six league games without a single victory. A 2-2 draw at Dean Court against Colchester was followed up by a 2-1 defeat at Port Vale, with Defoe stretching what must have seemed like a goal drought to three games. He was back on the scoresheet in another 2-2 home draw with promotion rivals Walsall, making it two goals in two outings against the Saddlers with two different clubs. But it was to be a bittersweet day for the striker.

After Eddie Howe had given the Cherries the lead, Defoe looked to have put his side in the driving seat with a powerful drive on 33 minutes. But it was his misdemeanour that allowed Walsall to get back into the game when he made a clumsy challenge in the area on Paul Hall just before the hour mark. Former Barcelona forward Ronnie Ekelund took full advantage as he fired home from the spot. It was the first time Defoe had fallen victim to lack of experience, and things got worse for the teenager when his thumping close range volley was somehow tipped away by goalkeeper Walker. A frustrating day for the hosts was confirmed when Darren Byfield grabbed a last-gasp equaliser to leave Defoe and his team crestfallen.

Late goals were becoming a feature of games involving Bournemouth. They were lucky to come away from Swindon with a point when an 85th minute leveller from Richard Hughes salvaged a 1-1 draw, before a late winner for Oldham at Boundary Park condemned the Cherries to defeat. But Defoe's personal disappointment was tempered somewhat by what can only be described as the inevitable.

With such impressive form at first-team level, it was only a matter of time before England came calling. To begin with it was the under-18 national team who wanted Defoe to play, against the Netherlands at Broadhall Way in Stevenage. A record-equalling run of goals seemed like the perfect way for Defoe to gain the national recognition his endeavours had deserved. As luck would have it, he had to miss out on Bournemouth's next game to play for England the following day. Unfortunately the south coast club could not give Defoe the send-off they wanted as Richard Hughes's missed penalty contributed to a 2-1 defeat at home to Bristol Rovers. Typically, Defoe would be back on the scoresheet when he took to the field for England as they drew 1-1 with their Dutch counterparts.

His return to Division Two came as an unused substitute the following Saturday as O'Driscoll opted to give his young striker a rest. However, his services were not called upon as the Cherries got back to winning ways with a 2-0 win at home to Brentford. Unfortunately, when Defoe did return to the starting line-up for Bournemouth's trip to south Yorkshire to take on Rotherham, the 18-year-old had what can only be described as a nightmare, giving the Millers a helping hand as they coasted to a comfortable 3-1 win. First, he gave away a needless free-kick in a dangerous position which allowed Kevin Watson to cross for Alan Lee's opener on the stroke of half-time. He then missed three wonderful chances to equalise after the break as a double from Mark Robins put the game beyond Bournemouth, who had only James Hayter's late consolation to show for the long trip north.

However, again Defoe's problem was simply inexperience at this level. There was no doubting his quality, as he proved in the very next game. While he did not get himself a goal, his hard work for the team meant he was able to create two goals for his team-mates as Bournemouth stormed back with a 4-0 demolition of Bristol City at Dean Court. After Wade Elliott had opened the scoring, Defoe's trickery earned a free-kick on the edge of the box that Richard Hughes stroked home for the second. A thumping volley from Carl Fletcher made it three in the first half, before Defoe's second contribution after the break. Robins goalkeeper Steve Phillips looked to have a routine clearance until the hard-working Defoe used his energy to chase the lost cause and charge down Phillips's attempted long ball, allowing Elliott to roll in his second and Bournemouth's fourth.

After a 1-1 draw at fellow playoff hopefuls Wigan, Defoe was back in the goals with the winner at Dean Court in a 1-0 victory over Bury. The Shakers looked to be in control of the game in the early stages but missed chance after chance after chance. They were made to pay by a young man who rarely needed to be asked twice. In the 21st minute a mistake from Chris Armstrong allowed him time and space in the box to hammer a shot through keeper Paddy Kenny, whose touch could only help the ball on its way into the net. It was Defoe's 15th goal of the season.

Two more victories would pass before Defoe got on the scoresheet again. First, a 3-0 victory at struggling Swansea, and then a 4-3 win at home to Oxford. It seemed strange that Defoe did not find the net in two high-scoring affairs, but the two victories were crucial to Bournemouth's push for the play-offs and the teenager knew that points on the board were the most important thing.

Heading into the final seven games, Defoe knew he needed to get back to his free-scoring ways. Any let up in Bournemouth's form between now and the end of the season would surely destroy any hopes of making the play-offs and winning a place in Division One via the final at Cardiff's Millennium Stadium. Of those seven remaining fixtures, four would be at home. While Bournemouth had received plaudits all season for their away form, it had been at Dean Court where Defoe had excelled with most of his goals. But if Bournemouth wanted to go up, they would need to pick up results at home, and see more of Defoe on the road if they were to achieve what had seemed like an impossible dream when he'd moved to the south coast back in October.

Reading were their next opponents. The Royals were flying high in the league and had serious promotion aspirations of their own as they took to the field at Dean Court. This was the perfect opportunity for Bournemouth to really show their credentials against a team they could well be facing again in the play-offs. Not only that, it was a home fixture, making this the perfect opportunity for Defoe to take advantage of his comfort zone after two games without finding the net.

All it took was three minutes for Defoe to do just that. Both teams were under immense pressure as this was a game of such importance. Neither side could afford to make a mistake as the punishment would be severe indeed. Unfortunately for Reading, a mistake is exactly what they made. Sammy Igoe looked to play an early backpass to his goalkeeper but it was hopelessly misjudged, allowing Defoe to race on to the loose ball and fire Bournemouth into the lead. But that was as good as it got for the hosts as the pressure to perform in front of their own fans got to them.

As well as Defoe had been doing in front of goal, Reading had two strikers who had been on fire all season in Jamie Cureton and Martin Butler, and it was this pair who put paid to Bournemouth's hopes in this game. A goal apiece in the space of five minutes showed exactly why Reading were at the right end of the table. Cureton levelled with a tap-in to make it 24 goals for the season, before Butler controlled his long ball to divert home his 22nd. Bournemouth did everything they could but could not find a way through, hitting the woodwork three times before Richard Hughes saw his penalty saved by Phil Whitehead.

So once more Bournemouth had to perform away from home and once again they did the business without Defoe scoring. A pair of headers from Steve Fletcher ensured they got back on track quickly with a 2-0 win at Notts County. Dean Court's next encounter would be against Stoke, the side against whom Defoe had scored on his Cherries debut and, more importantly, another top-of-the-table rival. Back at home, Defoe managed to find the net again with what turned out to be the winning goal. After 37 minutes of a dreary encounter he took advantage of a shocking error from Potters goalkeeper Gavin Ward. Ward's attempted clearance was cut out by Defoe on the edge of the penalty area and he volleyed home his 17th goal of the season in style.

However, Sean O'Driscoll was less than satisfied with the young man's overall performance. 'It was a great finish by Jermain, in a way similar to so many goals he has scored for us,' he said, 'but it was the only thing he did all night. He is a wonderful finisher and it was typical of him, but we could have done with more from him in other areas.' In a way this criticism was an indirect compliment. Because Defoe had shown how good he was in the preceding games, it was more noticeable when he did not offer as much as his manager knew he was capable of.

Defoe being what he is, he took his manager's constructive words in his stride. He appreciated he was still learning the game and knew that if he put the advice into practice it would only benefit him and the team, particularly with a crucial game at Peterborough on the horizon. Now was the time for him to find the net on the road – specifically, London Road.

After Andy Clarke had given the home side the lead it looked as though Bournemouth's hopes of reaching the play-offs were all but dashed. But Warren Feeney was on hand to restore parity and keep them alive and just three minutes later, Defoe put any doubts about his overall contribution to the team to rest with an imperious finish. Former Arsenal and Northern Ireland midfielder Steve Morrow slipped 15 yards from goal, allowing the nippy striker to take the ball and rifle a fine angled drive across goalkeeper Mark Tyler and just inside the far post, causing manager O'Driscoll to leap from the bench in a moment of pure elation. His words of wisdom to the pint-sized striker had had the desired effect.

England under-18 duty again upset Defoe's first-team run, as a trip to Poland forced him out of Bournemouth's crucial home game against Wycombe. But Feeney, on loan from Leeds United, deputised admirably and was among the goals for the second game in a row to open the scoring. Wade Elliott added the second to keep Bournemouth ticking over. For Defoe, it would be a disappointing night in Gdansk as young England could only manage a 0-0 draw and thus failed to qualify for the European Championship.

Elliott would again score for Bournemouth in their next game, against Northampton at Dean Court, with Claus Jorgensen grabbing a second to set things up nicely for a do-or-die encounter with Reading at the Madejski Stadium. If Bournemouth could go there and win, they would reach the play-offs. Anything else simply would not do. Failure to secure all three points would bring to an end Defoe's time on the south coast. Defoe did manage to score his 20th of the season, but it would prove to be his last as it and two strikes from Elliott were cancelled out by Darren Caskey, Martin Butler and Nicky Forster. The 3-3 draw meant that Bournemouth finished in seventh place – one place outside the play-off spots.

It was a deflating end to what had turned into a fantastic season for both Defoe and Bournemouth. His 20 goals had fired them into play-off contention and it was only on the last day of the season that they had finally been forced out of the race. But for Defoe it was just the beginning. 'The club has helped me a lot,' he said of his temporary home after the game. Sean O'Driscoll was quick to heap praise on the boy who had grown up with every game into a striker with the potential to go all the way. O'Driscoll made a clear suggestion to Hammers boss Harry Redknapp. 'I'd play Jermain,' he said.

'He'll score goals at any level.' If there was one positive for Defoe to take from a disappointing end to the Division Two season, it was that he would be back at West Ham in time for the final game of the Premier League campaign, giving him an early chance to have a crack at the top flight.

However, by the time Defoe returned to Upton Park, Redknapp was no longer in charge – a dispute with Hammers chairman Terry Brown had seen West Ham and their manager part company. The reins had been taken up by former coach Glenn Roeder, who had been brought to the club by Redknapp in 1999. Fortunately for Defoe he was coming back to a manager who knew him from their time together with West Ham's reserves before his move south. He knew the new boss had an idea of what he was all about, and he was named in Roeder's squad for the final game of the season, against Middlesbrough at the Riverside.

The game was effectively a dead rubber. West Ham's poor end to the season had left them clear of the relegation zone but some way from the top half of the table, while Middlesbrough had managed to stave off relegation in a season when far more had been expected of them. Defoe watched from the bench as the hosts took the lead through Cameroon international Joseph-Desire Job's first goal in English football. Joe Cole inspired West Ham to an equaliser when his nimble footwork mesmerised the home defence and allowed him to feed Svetoslav Todorov, who scored his first West Ham goal. French World Cup winner Christian Karembeu then drove beyond Shaka Hislop to claim all three points for the hosts, but it was still a proud day for Defoe as he took to the field with 22 minutes remaining to make his Premier League debut. Admittedly his contribution was limited, but it was a significant moment for the teenager who had made it to the top flight within two seasons as a professional.

But the season was about to get even better for Defoe. His exceptional form for Bournemouth, coupled with his first-team breakthrough at West Ham, brought the reward of a place in Howard Wilkinson's England under-21 squad for a friendly international against Mexico at Leicester City's old Filbert Street stadium. 'It was a bit scary, but exciting too,' he recalled of his selection. 'Most of the other guys were playing regularly for Premiership teams and here I was being thrown in at the deep end.'

But again Defoe would let his football do the talking. He was involved in England's opening goal as his second-half effort was parried by Mexican keeper Armando Navarrete into the path of Derby's Malcolm Christie, who made no mistake from close range. And with 17 minutes left Defoe got himself yet another debut goal – the third of his short career – as a quick turn and shot put the result beyond doubt for England. Jay Bothroyd of Coventry added a third six minutes from time to cap an impressive night for England's youngsters. For Defoe, it was a fine way to introduce himself to the wider international stage.

As 2000/01 drew to a close, it had been a season to remember for Jermain Defoe. His second year as a professional had given him an introduction to regular first-team football, a record-equalling goalscoring run in the Football League, an inspiring fight for the playoffs, a Premier League debut, the beginnings of an international career, a goal in every debut he'd made and a total of more than 20 goals. And all this before his 19th birthday. It was clear for all to see that Defoe was ready to make the step up and take the top division in English football by storm.

Chapter 3

Hammer Time

2001/02 would be another landmark season for Jermain Defoe, being his first season of regular Premier League squad membership. But before any dreams of top-flight glory could be realised, the teenager had more work to do on the international stage.

As he'd made a goal-scoring start to his England under-21 career, it came as no surprise that Defoe was again involved as the national team's younger equivalent took to the field in June for a crucial European Championship qualifier in Greece. Unfortunately, it would not be a game to remember for Defoe as England crashed to a disappointing defeat in what became a bad-tempered encounter at the Athens home of Panathinaikos.

Playing in front of the England senior team coach Sven-Göran Eriksson, Defoe struggled to make an impact on the game as Howard Wilkinson's men fell a goal behind to a header from Dimitris Papadopoulos. They then found themselves two goals down moments before the interval when Giorgos Vakouftsis swept home. At half-time Wilkinson felt the need to make a change and, somewhat surprisingly given England needed a goal, replaced Defoe with Arsenal winger Jermaine Pennant.

With a two-goal deficit and an in-form striker back on the bench, England were in serious trouble and things went from bad to worse as the situation descended into a farce for the visitors. Defoe's West Ham team-mate goalkeeper Stephen Bywater inexplicably allowed Chelsea centre-half John Terry's header back to slither through his grasp to make it three for the hosts. The saying goes 'beware of Greeks bearing gifts', but there was only side in a giving mood that night.

Just as it looked as if Defoe's misfortune on the night was spreading to his West Ham club mates, the increasingly impressive Michael Carrick looked to have thrown the Three Lions a lifeline with a lovely 25-yard strike that zipped into the Greek net. However, that was as good as it got for the visitors as the mood on the pitch deteriorated rapidly.

First, Tottenham's Luke Young was shown a red card for shoving Giorgos Theodoridis in retaliation for what he felt was a foul. Then Terry's bad night was compounded when he too was given his marching orders after succumbing to his frustrations with a two-footed lunge on Dimitris Salpigidis. After that there was no way back for England. A total loss of control ensued and on the final whistle the inevitable melee developed. Wilkinson was seen restraining Blackburn midfielder David Dunn as his team gave in to their anger.

It was to be Wilkinson's last game in charge of the under-21s as he resigned to make way for David Platt. The former England midfielder and captain did not have to wait long for his first game in charge, a home fixture against Holland at Reading's Madejski Stadium just before the start of the season in mid-August.

In the space of two seasons, Defoe had already been required to impress four managers – Harry Redknapp, Sean O'Driscoll, Glenn Roeder and Howard Wilkinson. Now a fifth man would need to see what the young Hammer could do. He may only have been 18 years old but all of a sudden Defoe was back in a very familiar situation. He knew how to respond to situations like these. He would do exactly what he had done on previous occasions. He would score.

The problem, however, was that after Defoe's comparatively poor showing in Greece, Platt had decided to leave him on the bench, opting instead for Aston Villa marksman Darius Vassell, who already had a fair number of Premier League appearances under his belt. It proved to be a shrewd move from the new coach as Vassell thumped England into the lead with a cracking long-range effort after just six minutes. An injury meant that Vassell was unable to come out for the second half, but Platt had the perfect replacement waiting in the wings.

Anything Vassell could do, Defoe could do quicker. Three minutes of play was all it needed for him to remind everybody exactly what he was all about. He reacted quickest to a loose ball at the far post to score with his very first touch, doubling England's lead. It was trademark Defoe – and it said it all that a boy with just one first-team season under his belt already had a trademark. He was not finished either, as he set up Malcolm Christie for England's third three minutes from time before rounding off the scoring himself in the last minute. It was the perfect way to impress the new coach. And with Wilkinson watching from the stands, it was perhaps the perfect way to show the old coach how things could have been.

Normally, an international fixture just days before the start of the season is the last thing most managers, and some players, would want. But for Defoe, his busy pre-season of England representation had shown his West Ham manager Glenn Roeder that he was definitely ready for first-team action. Unlike the last season, there was less competition for a place in the starting line-up, Davor Suker having left Upton Park to join German outfit 1860 Munich. That left the regular strike partnership of Frederic Kanoute and Paolo Di Canio and January signing Svetoslav Todorov as the only men ahead of Defoe in the pecking order up front. And with Kanoute injured at the start of the season, Defoe was up to third in line.

However, while Roeder was certainly impressed with what Defoe had to offer, he was not prepared to throw his young charge in at the deep end right away. The manager himself was relatively inexperienced and knew that if he was to win over the dressing room he would need to keep the more established professionals happy before turning to younger talent. That said, he knew the qualities Defoe possessed and made sure he was involved with the first team from the start, giving him a place on the bench for the first game of the season, against Liverpool at Anfield.

With only a mid-table finish to show for a difficult 2000/01 season, West Ham were under some pressure to improve. With a rookie manager at the helm, there was widespread expectation that the Hammers would be in the relegation mix this time around, particularly after experiencing some significant losses in player personnel. Rio Ferdinand had joined Leeds and Frank Lampard had moved across London to Chelsea, ripping the spine out of a comparatively young side. A trip to one of the title contenders was never going to be easy, and under these circumstances the task looked positively gargantuan.

It came as little surprise when West Ham were beaten 2-1, but their performance was encouraging. They more than matched Liverpool in the first half, but it was the quality of another young English striker, Michael Owen, that eventually put them to the sword with a goal either side of Paolo Di Canio's equaliser from the penalty spot. Defoe did not enter the fray until the 72nd minute when he replaced Todorov seven minutes before Owen's winner, but he did enough in his 18 minutes to suggest the Premier League was the right level for him. He even had half a chance to give the Londoners the lead shortly after coming on but his sharpness was just lacking.

Defoe's lively Anfield cameo was not enough to earn him a starting place for West Ham's first home game of the season, against Leeds United. Again he was restricted to just 20 minutes on the pitch, again in the place of the Bulgarian Todorov. Rio Ferdinand captained Leeds on his return to Upton Park and it was in no small part down to his strong performance that the Hammers forwards got little change out of their Yorkshire opponents in a 0-0 draw. Roeder said after the game that he was still determined to bring in new faces and that Defoe was by no means ready to start on a regular basis. With Mali striker Kanoute yet to return, the manager was adamant the teenager would be restricted to cameos for the time being.

So once again Defoe had a job on his hands to prove something to his manager. Another England Under-21 game was on the horizon, this time against lowly Albania in a

European Championship qualifier at Middlesbrough's Riverside Stadium – the site of Defoe's Premier League debut. Rewarded with a start by David Platt after his impressive second half last time out, Defoe made sure his contribution would be noticed, even if the show would be stolen by new Arsenal signing Francis Jeffers, who notched a hat-trick.

It was Defoe who laid on two of the Merseysider's goals. Firstly he released Jeffers with a pass down the right channel for the Arsenal man to stroke home, before pulling the ball back low and hard across the box for Jeffers to double his and England's score. Defoe then got the goal he deserved after being slipped through by Scott Parker, racing on to the pass and slotting home with a coolness that belied his frustration at being left on the bench for his club. Jonathan Greening made it four before Jeffers completed his treble for a thumping 5-0 win to put England back in the qualification picture.

But it was still not enough to get Defoe a place in the starting XI back at his club. West Ham's trip to Pride Park to face Derby was another frustrating affair for both player and team as they endured their second goalless draw in a row. Again Defoe would only be introduced as a late replacement, this time with only ten minutes to make an impact. He almost did just that with two chances to grab the points but saw his first shot fly just wide and his second well blocked by a stubborn Rams defence. However, the words of his manager in the aftermath were telling: 'I dare say that he will get starts during the season but we need to strengthen him up during the year, make his upper body strength better. He will get lots of experience training with the first team every day and coming on from the bench and hopefully his first goal isn't too far away. He is probably all about next year.' Defoe would see about that.

Roeder stayed true to his word and Defoe was rewarded with his first start of the season – his full debut in the West Ham first team. It came in a League Cup tie against Reading at the Madejski Stadium, where he had recently scored for England under-21s. However, this was not to be a happy return for a striker who was still desperate to impress. He had a number of chances to make the breakthrough for his side but things just would not go his way. His first chance came after being put through by Trevor Sinclair and jinking between two defenders but his shot was brilliantly blocked by Royals keeper Phil Whitehead. West Ham were dominant and continued to create chances, with Don Hutchison and Sinclair both going close before Defoe had another two chances to give his team the lead. Again he could not find a way past Whitehead.

Both sides continued to create chances as the home side gradually found a foothold in the game, but it was no surprise when 90 minutes and extra time elapsed with neither side able to find the net. The lottery of penalties would be the only way to separate these two sides. Almost as significantly, it was West Ham's third 0-0 draw in a row. They were without a goal in open play all season.

As the shoot-out progressed, Reading's fourth penalty taker James Harper saw his effort saved by Hammers keeper Shaka Hislop, giving Defoe the chance to wrap up the win. It was a crucial moment for a team that badly needed a win, and a player who badly wanted to impress. However, the teenager could only fire his penalty onto the post and the initiative was handed back to Reading. Scott Minto missed West Ham's next penalty, allowing Adrian Viveash to slot home the decisive kick for the Second Division outfit. It was an embarrassing night for West Ham, and a heartbreaker for Defoe.

As the frustrating start to the season began to get to the youngster, his irritation begin to manifest itself. Ahead of West Ham's trip to Middlesbrough he spoke to the media about it being a good time to take on the North-Easterners who, like their London counterparts, had yet to win a game this season. However, what seemed like an innocuous comment only served to rile up Boro, who came flying out of the blocks to win the game 2-0. Their captain, former West Ham star Paul Ince, summed up the situation. 'We were sitting around the training ground with the papers and we read Jermain Defoe said it was the best time to be playing us. I, for one, wouldn't let a young player go around saying that. It gave us a gee-up. Jermain is a kid – it's not really his fault. For the last two weeks everyone, bar our own fans, has been having a go at us.'

For Defoe it was an eye-opener as to how powerful the media can be for Premier League footballers, both for and against. The game itself was a strange one for Defoe, who was given a longer spell on the pitch than usual, coming on for Cameroon defender Rigobert Song at half-time after West Ham had gifted the hosts two goals. Again Defoe looked lively throughout the second half but, as Ince put it bluntly, 'West Ham weren't up for it.'

Next up was a home game against Newcastle, and with Frederic Kanoute fit again after injury, Defoe was back on the bench. It looked as though a place in the starting line-up was as far away as ever, particularly as with the long-legged striker back on board, West Ham finally chalked up their first win of the season. Kanoute himself rounded things off after Don Hutchison's strike and a sublime individual goal from Di Canio, giving the Hammers a 3-0 win. Things were finally starting to look positive at Upton Park, but Defoe still had to wait for his first Hammers goal of the season.

He was not involved in West Ham's next game, a disastrous 5-0 defeat by Everton at Goodison Park, so again it would be down to Defoe's international form to bring him back into the thoughts of his club management. The England under-21s' return match against the Greek side that had so embarrassed them in Athens was the perfect opportunity to show his mental strength. A win was required to reach a qualifying play-off and a win was what England got, thanks in part to the goal from Defoe that set them on their way. Malcolm Christie scored the second as England clinched a 2-1 victory.

Despite Defoe getting back among the goals, Roeder still refused to give him a starting place in the West Ham team, and in the two fixtures that followed he would not get on the pitch at all. He was an unused substitute for a dismal trip to Blackburn Rovers, where Michael Carrick scored West Ham's only goal as they were crushed 7-1, their heaviest defeat of the season by a long way. He was left out again for the next game, a 2-0 win at home to Southampton, where Kanoute looked to be cementing his place as a regular partner for Di Canio with both goals.

West Ham were at home in their next game as well, in a huge London derby against Chelsea. With Frank Lampard set to make an emotional return to the club the fans felt he had turned his back on, and his new club enjoying an unbeaten start to the season, tensions were running high at the Boleyn Ground. Defoe was once again named among the substitutes, but he would get more than his fair share of the action.

The hosts flew out of the blocks and Carrick grabbed a goal after just five minutes with a smart finish following quick build-up from Sebastien Schemmel and Trevor Sinclair. Chelsea were shell-shocked and eight minutes later they found themselves two down as Kanoute made it three goals in two games with a low strike into the bottom corner from 20 yards. All of a sudden West Ham's season was back on track.

Jimmy Floyd Hasselbaink hauled Chelsea back into the game before the break with a thumping drive, but Roeder decided to go for broke and threw Defoe into the fray at the interval. Despite not having been involved for two games, the striker was straight into the action and nearly extended West Ham's lead with his very first involvement. He raced beyond the Blues defence to latch on to a Kanoute flick, but while his guided effort beat the outstretched arm of keeper Mark Bosnich, it also beat the post.

However the miss would not prove decisive as the Hammers held on for a huge victory to set them up for a tough fixture against struggling Ipswich Town at Portman Road. West Ham had conceded 12 goals in their last two away games and were in danger of letting their away form keep them at the wrong end of the table. Defoe did not get on to the pitch until the 88th minute, but it was to be a momentous day for him nonetheless. Di Canio gave the visitors the lead after 21 minutes with their first real attack of the game, only to see his goal pegged back by Hermann Hreidarsson's close-range volley.

Kanoute restored West Ham's lead with 18 minutes to go as his effort deflected off Hreidarsson and into the net before Di Canio was replaced by Defoe with two minutes to go. His injury-time contribution was to be a telling one. He robbed Ipswich defender Thomas Gaardsoe of the ball to leave him one on one with goalkeeper Matteo Sereni before calmly rolling the ball home to increase West Ham's lead to two goals. More importantly, he had finally scored his first Premier League goal.

Matt Holland pulled a goal back for the hosts shortly afterwards but it did not prevent the Hammers grabbing their first away win of the season. And it certainly did not take any shine off the day for Defoe. He had finally scored in the top flight and in doing so had guaranteed three crucial points for his team, proving to his manager that he could make a real difference to West Ham's faltering form. After a spell with no involvement on the pitch at all, he had shown he was worthy of his place. The next step was to prove to Roeder that he was ready to play from the start every week.

That, unfortunately, would have to wait as West Ham's return to Upton Park saw Defoe back on the subs' bench against big-spending Premier League new boys Fulham. The hosts were confident going into the game after three wins in a row in October had catapulted them up the table to 11th. But Fulham made comfortable work of things with goals from French imports Sylvain Legwinski and Steed Malbranque to claim a 2-0 win. Defoe made his bow with 28 minutes to go and nearly got his side back in the game with a neat turn and shot but Holland keeper Edwin van der Sar was equal to it. But again Defoe had shown he was able to make an impact, and the Hammers' next game was a trip to the Valley to play Charlton – the club where it had all started for him. It was a game in which Defoe was desperate to feature. First, however, was the small matter of an under-21 European Championship qualifier against Holland.

Although the European Championship was a more immediate concern, as it was due to start at the end of the season, the England players knew that an impressive showing sooner rather than later could give them an extra push towards the full squad. And with a World Cup coming the following June, impressing Sven-Göran Eriksson was high on the agenda for those after a seat on the plane to Japan and South Korea. Unfortunately, Defoe would have a quiet play-off against the Dutch. He played the entire 90 minutes of the first leg in Utrecht but failed to score as David Dunn and Sean Davis helped England to a 2-2 draw. The second leg at Pride Park would be triumphant for England as Defoe's West Ham team-mate Carrick scored the only goal to send them to the finals. Although things had not gone to plan on an individual level for Defoe, the experience of playing against such big names of the future as Dirk Kuyt, Rafael van der Vaart and Andy van der Meyde would stand him in good stead for a senior international career.

But international football was the last thing on Defoe's mind as he made his first return to the Valley since becoming a member of the West Ham first team. He had been given his share of verbal abuse from fans when he had played there in a reserve game for the Hammers, but it was to be far louder this time. Despite his improving form, Defoe was again on the bench. Perhaps manager Glenn Roeder was trying to protect his young starlet from the taunts and jeers that were coming his way from the stands. However, with Kanoute injured again it was a strange choice to leave out Defoe in favour of Paul Kitson, who had not scored in the Premier League since March 1999.

It turned out to be an inspired choice. Kitson gave the visitors the lead after just three minutes before a double from Jason Euell turned the game on its head. But Kitson made it a brace apiece with his second after half an hour. Charlton took the lead again six minutes into the second half through Jonatan Johansson before Kitson stunned everybody in the stadium with a close-range finish to round off his hat-trick in the 64th minute. Kitson left the field with 12 minutes to go and was replaced by the man who had left Charlton with the sole purpose of developing his career. Enter Jermain Defoe to a cacophony of boos from the home support. It was hard enough coming on for a man who had just scored three times, never mind coming on for a man who had just scored three times with nearly everyone in the ground giving you an earful. This was pressure.

Pressure? What pressure? The 19-year-old took a little under ten minutes to show just why the Addicks faithful were so furious about seeing him playing somewhere else. The booing and jeering was the natural reaction from fans who would love to have someone in their team with his eye for goal. With just two minutes left, a cross from Christian Dailly took a mean deflection and dropped in the area to the young man who simply thrived on such situations. Defoe dispatched a deft close-range strike to score what was surely the winning goal. Surely he had guaranteed emerging from his Valley return with the last laugh.

Unfortunately football has a funny habit of coming back to bite you, and so it proved in stoppage time as Johansson replaced the home crowd's boos with a rapturous roar at his breathtaking overhead kick – one of the goals of the season. It was a phenomenal game, summed up perfectly by John Cross in the *Mirror*: 'Throw into the mix West Ham supersub Jermain Defoe stepping off the bench to haunt the club he controversially snubbed to sign for the Hammers when he was a schoolboy. Yes, for sheer excitement, goals and kamikaze defending, this match had absolutely everything.' While his goal had not proved to be the winner after all, Defoe had exorcised a personal demon and, more importantly, he would finally be rewarded with a starting role and his full Premier League debut.

Tottenham Hotspur were the visitors to Upton Park for the fixture, the Hammers' third London derby in a row. With Paolo Di Canio and Frederic Kanoute both out, and Kitson and Defoe both on goal-scoring form, the starting strikers picked themselves. However, without the creativity of Di Canio and the power of Kanoute, it was always going to be difficult for the Hammers against a solid Spurs outfit. Defoe's best chance of the game came late in the first half but he was unable to finish a chance that Joe Cole had expertly created. That was about as good as it got for the Hammers as Tottenham gradually took control of the game. Spurs missed scoring opportunity after scoring opportunity before Les Ferdinand eventually slammed home the rebound after David James had made an excellent save from Gus Poyet's header four minutes into the second half. It was the only goal of the game.

This latest frustrating defeat led to West Ham slipping further down the table to 15th. The inconsistent form that had plagued their early season was back with a vengeance and in danger of pulling them into a relegation dogfight. Things were not helped at the start of December with another defeat, again by a single goal, this time by Sunderland at the Stadium of Light. However, Defoe started the game and while he did not get on the scoresheet, he caught the eye with a strong performance, going close on two occasions. He should have scored in the first half but with only the goalkeeper to beat he fired wide, before being slipped through by Cole only to see keeper Thomas Sorensen make a good save. After the game Roeder commented, 'Jermain Defoe got into some excellent positions and will be an excellent goalscorer in years to come. But today was not his day.' Little did he know, Defoe's day would come a great deal sooner than he thought.

Paolo Di Canio came back into the Hammers side for the visit of Aston Villa but took the place of Kitson, allowing Defoe to keep his starting berth. With a trip to champions Manchester United on the horizon, it was crucial that they picked up something against a Villa side who had looked far more solid in their early-season endeavours. But in the very first minute of the game a bad clearance from former Villa keeper David James went straight to Steve Stone, who crossed for Dion Dublin to open the scoring. Defoe saw a header saved by Peter Enckelman as he led the Hammers charge for an equaliser before the break.

They would have to wait a lot longer than that, especially as the usually dependable Di Canio missed with a weak penalty after Defoe had been felled in the box by Steve Staunton. It seemed that if West Ham were going to come away from this game with anything, then Defoe would have to take matters into his own hands. And deep into stoppage time he did just that, racing onto a hopeful long ball to thunder it past Enckelman and steal a point that the Londoners scarcely deserved.

That goal was rewarded with another start in the club's biggest game of the season so far. Games against Manchester United at Old Trafford are never easy at the best of times, so with a barren run of no wins in their past five games to show, it is fair to say West Ham were definitely the underdogs.

However, with Paolo Di Canio in the side again anything was possible, as he had proved the previous season with the only goal in an FA Cup tie between the two sides on the same ground. Lightning would strike twice, but it was not to be the Italian who dealt the fatal blow.

As expected, United started the game strongly and created a host of chances that should have been enough to kill off the opposition. But they were uncharacteristically wasteful in front of goal and slowly but surely the visitors got themselves into the game and started to put pressure on Fabien Barthez's goal. Finally, just after the hour mark, West Ham stunned Old Trafford by breaking the deadlock. Sebastien Schemmel found Di Canio on the right wing, the mercurial Italian crossed to the far post and there was Defoe. Despite his lack of height, he rose majestically above Phil Neville to loop a perfect header off the crossbar and over the line. It was a goal that showed he was on his way to becoming the complete striker – an ability to finish from close range, long range, with either foot or with his head. And on the biggest Premier League stage of them all.

Yet even this was not enough to keep Defoe in the team, as Kanoute's return to fitness meant he was back on the bench for the visit to Upton Park of Arsenal, the club he had supported as a boy. But again, the manager's team selection was vindicated when the French-born forward scored with a confident strike in the first half, only for it to be cancelled out by Defoe's fellow young England hopeful Ashley Cole. A thigh strain curtailed Kanoute's game at the interval, leading him to make way for Defoe for the second half, and leaving a place in the team for the youngster in the next game at Leicester.

A win against reigning champions Manchester United

followed by a draw with the title-chasing Gunners showed West Ham were certainly capable of pushing themselves up the Premier League table. In Di Canio, Kanoute and now Defoe they had a genuine goal threat, with all three sharing the scoring between them. Unfortunately, with continuing injury problems for Kanoute it was difficult for the front line to form any kind of consistency.

Even more unfortunately, the club was going through a turbulent time in the press after the drunken antics of some squad members at the team's Christmas party showed them in a very bad light. Australian defender Hayden Foxe was caught urinating on the bar at London's Sugar Reef nightclub while another player vomited in the VIP area and another had a barman in a headlock.

With such behaviour going on off the pitch, it was little surprise that there was not much to cheer on it. Despite great results against the two main title contenders, West Ham never got going against Leicester at Filbert Street. Senrab graduate Muzzy Izzet gave the Foxes the lead just before the break with a deflected effort, and it took a cheeky Di Canio penalty to restore parity, but only after Leicester captain Matt Elliott had done little to help football's struggling reputation by receiving a straight red card for head-butting Trevor Sinclair. Defoe played 88 minutes before being substituted, but his most telling contribution was a crucial goal line clearance after keeper David James had failed to deal with an Andrew Impey corner.

Defoe and the Hammers were in need of a Christmas present but they had to wait until Boxing Day to get it. In a thumping win at home to Derby the striker returned to his role as a supersub with devastating effect. The hosts got off to a flying start when Sebastien Schemmel scored in the first five minutes. They did not score again until the last 15 minutes, but with Derby looking to retrieve the game for their first away win of the season, it was no shock to see the Hammers score three more in the latter stages. Di Canio's smart finish was followed by a stunning strike by Sinclair, whose mid-air scissor kick proved to be one of the goals of the season. Defoe appeared shortly after Di Canio's goal and he rounded off the scoring with two minutes left, prodding home Carrick's pass for his fifth goal of the season.

Di Canio was suspended for Liverpool's visit to the Boleyn in the last fixture of 2001 so Defoe found himself back in the team. His performance was one to remember as he showed he could offer more to the team than his goals. First he was responsible for the opening goal, scored by Sinclair, as he powered into the area and squared for the England winger just before Swiss defender Stephane Henchoz clattered into him. He then had a couple of chances to double his side's advantage when a quick turn and shot brought the best out of keeper Jerzy Dudek, and a shot from Sinclair's cross flew wide. The missed chances would prove costly as Michael Owen stole the headlines with his 100th goal for Liverpool.

England boss Sven-Göran Eriksson was at Elland Road to cast his eye over the English contingent as West Ham began 2002 with their first defeat in seven games, a run that had taken them back up to mid-table. Unfortunately Defoe would not be one of the names to impress as Leeds cruised to a 3-0 victory, his only real chance being a header that he glanced wide. Still, he retained a starting place for the FA Cup third-round tie at Macclesfield Town.

It proved to be something of a virtuoso performance from the under-21 starlet, with two goals that booked West Ham' place in the hat for round four. He opened the scoring on the stroke of half-time as his unerring determination took him in front of his man to flick the ball into the bottom corner. He grabbed his second in the 77th minute after a quick exchange of passes with Don Hutchison left him to steer home right-footed. Joe Cole scored a lovely individual goal to seal the win but it was Defoe who came away as man of the match. The manager was again delighted with Defoe's efforts. 'Jermain is building himself a reputation, proving he can score in the Premiership,' said Roeder. 'And there will be a lot more to come.'

Normally words like that would put pressure on a young player but Defoe's self-confidence was understandably sky high. 'Injuries have given me a chance,' he said after the game. 'The manager told me at the start of the season I would be the first in line if that was the case. There is pressure on me but it makes it easier when you have great players around you and I'm still young. I was delighted with my goals today and I hope there are plenty more to come.'

Despite Roeder's positive comments at Moss Rose, he reverted to picking Defoe as a substitute for the next five games, starting with a home win against Leicester. Di Canio volleyed the only goal before being replaced by Defoe, whom the experienced Italian gave plenty of advice as he left the field. It was evidence of the learning environment afforded to young players at West Ham. It had clearly rubbed off on the Hammers talisman, who was quick to offer his young strike partner the benefit of his know-how – something that was to help Defoe immensely as his career continued.

Di Canio was no stranger to scoring in big games, and it was a skill that he looked to have been teaching Defoe. The young Englishman had already scored a winning goal against

Manchester United, not to mention several late strikes to gain points when it looked as though his team would be leaving games without any. Again Defoe would find the net late on in a big game away at Chelsea, with a smart finish ten minutes after coming on for Kanoute. Unfortunately it was to little avail as Chelsea had already scored four, and added a fifth soon after his consolation in a game that saw Di Canio sent off.

A quirk in the fixture list saw West Ham making another trip to Stamford Bridge to for the fourth round of the FA Cup. Jimmy Floyd Hasselbaink gave Chelsea the lead after 20 minutes and it looked as though the Hammers would be in for more punishment. But a new resilience from the visitors was backed up by the introduction of Defoe for the last 25 minutes. His fresh, high-pace, high-intensity contribution helped tip the balance in the away side's favour, culminating in Kanoute's late equaliser to force a replay at Upton Park.

Before that, though, there were two more second-half cameos to be made. First, he played 24 minutes of West Ham's 2-0 defeat at St. Mary's against Southampton. While little of note happened for him on the pitch, off it he was made fully aware of where he stood at the club when Roeder confirmed that Di Canio would not be joining Manchester United – a transfer rumour that had been gathering momentum throughout the winter. While Di Canio had been nothing but a positive influence on Defoe, his departure would have created an opportunity for the teenager to claim a regular starting place.

Instead he was on the bench again against Blackburn at the Boleyn and able to see first hand exactly why the Italian forward was so crucial to the Hammers' cause. First he instigated a lovely move which culminated in Trevor Sinclair slotting home, before playing a stunning pass through the eye of a needle to Kanoute, who fired in from 20 yards to seal the points. Defoe would replace the injured Kanoute with 18 minutes to go and once again found himself in a position to score with his first touch, but American goalkeeper Brad Friedel made a fine save to keep the score as it was.

Next up was the FA Cup replay against Chelsea at Upton Park. Kanoute had not recovered from the knock he had picked up and Di Canio was beginning a three-match ban for his red card, so Defoe would make his return to the starting line-up. It was another great opportunity for him, again playing in front of the England coach who had come to see the likes of Trevor Sinclair, David James and Joe Cole. Again Mr Eriksson would be leaving with another name at the front of his mind.

It took 38 minutes for the future England front man to open the scoring in some style, launching himself into a stunning scissor kick that deflected the ball off England Under-21 team-mate John Terry and in via the crossbar. Add acrobatic to the kind of goals Defoe was capable of scoring.

Hasselbaink levelled for the Blues shortly before half-time with a rocket of a free-kick, but just six minutes into the second period Defoe became the toast of east London. Don Hutchison's shot was parried by keeper Carlo Cudicini, but the fox-in-the-box instincts of Defoe saw him perfectly placed to stab in the rebound from close range to restore West Ham's lead. But it was all to end in heartbreak for the Hammers as Mikael Forssell equalised and a thumping header from Terry settled the tie in injury time. It was not to be West Ham's season in the cup competitions.

With another start awarded, Defoe was keen to impress at Bolton's Reebok Stadium. A neat step-over almost set up Kanoute before his pace allowed Defoe to race on to a pass from Joe Cole, switch feet and unleash a low, powerful strike that keeper Jussi Jaaskelainen did extremely well to keep out. It was another strong performance from West Ham but ultimately it would end in another defeat by a single goal.

The defeat would keep the Hammers in mid-table but they finally made it into the top half with a 1-0 victory in their next home fixture against Middlesbrough. Defoe's contribution was somewhat muted, perhaps the result of an early accidental clash with defender Ugo Ehiogu that left the centre-back with a broken nose and stitches under his eye after just two minutes. It was to be another goalless afternoon for Defoe, after what was becoming his usual chance was well saved by the opposition goalkeeper.

Another disappointing day would follow at Villa Park where, despite another eye-catching performance, he was unable to score as the Hammers crashed to their tenth away defeat of the season. Just as Terry had done in the FA Cup, another of Defoe's fellow England under-21 internationals stole the victory with the very last action of the game. This time it was Darius Vassell who turned in a late, late cross to pinch the points.

No goals in three starts meant the writing was on the wall for Defoe when Kanoute and Di Canio were both ready for action again. He would be a substitute again for the visit of Everton, which saw the Hammers get back to winning ways, again by one goal to nil. Defoe only managed to get on to the pitch for the last six minutes as West Ham looked to have cemented their Premier League status after what had been an awful start to the season. While it was disappointing for the 19-year-old not to be playing, he knew full well that the most important thing was his team getting points on the board and staying in the top flight.

Next up for Defoe and his team was the visit of Manchester United to Upton Park. The Red Devils were still mindful of Defoe's shock winner at Old Trafford back in December and were probably pleased to see he was only listed among the substitutes. United were not prepared to let lightning strike twice as they looked to continue their Premier League title charge. Despite falling behind twice, they eventually cruised to a comprehensive 5-3 victory, but not before Defoe had emerged from the bench to net his team a consolation, after which England captain David Beckham rounded off the scoring from the penalty spot. Sven-Göran Eriksson was in town again but it looked as though the young Hammers on show were heading for the European Under-21 Championships in the summer rather than the big party in Japan and South Korea.

And so it proved as Defoe took the field again for England under-21s at Bradford's Valley Parade Stadium, taking on European Championship opponents Italy in a dress rehearsal. Defoe was involved in England's goal in a 1-1 draw as Gareth Barry's effort after a goalmouth scramble appeared to brush the striker's leg on its way into the net. There was little doubt in Defoe's mind that the goal was his, but it was awarded to Barry. Whoever got the credit, it was a good result against a side that had designs on winning the competition in Switzerland.

Back on league duty, Defoe made it three goals in three games with the clincher in a 3-1 home win over Ipswich Town – the team against whom he had scored his very first Premier

League goal at the end of October. After Paolo Di Canio had put West Ham 2-1 up, Defoe came off the bench and sealed the win with four minutes remaining when his low strike crept just inside the post. Again Roeder was delighted with his contribution, saying: 'Next year he will have a bigger role.' Surely that was music to the teenager's ears.

Two more wins for West Ham, albeit without Defoe's goalscoring touch, at Fulham and against Charlton, propelled them to the dizzying heights of seventh in the table. Defoe would not be on the scoresheet in the 1-1 draw at Spurs that followed but his performance having started the game was one that drew many plaudits and cemented his status as a star of the future. His showing against Sunderland at home the following weekend was not as impressive but that did not prevent him grabbing the final goal with a close range header in a 3-0 win to extend West Ham's unbeaten run to five matches, with only one defeat in their last seven.

As the season neared its end Defoe made a brief cameo from the bench in a 2-0 defeat at Highbury by champions-elect Arsenal. This was followed by starts in the last two games. At St. James' Park he scored the opening goal, only for Newcastle to claim a 3-1 win, before he played his part in the 2-1 win at home to Bolton which ensured the Hammers finished seventh in the table – the third-highest league finish in their history.

For Defoe it had been a landmark season. Despite it being his first in the top flight and despite never being a regular starter, he had still managed to finish the season with a remarkable haul of 14 goals. The feat was made all the more impressive as he ended the year as West Ham's top scorer in a squad that contained such established strikers as Di Canio and Kanoute. He had topped the scoring charts already and his manager had promised him a more prominent role in the season to come, although now he could hardly afford him anything else.

Before that, though, there was the small matter of the European Under-21 Championships. Defoe's scoring form for the England youngsters meant he was one of the first names on David Platt's squad list for the showpiece event in Switzerland at the end of the domestic season. However, it was not to be Defoe's – or England's – tournament.

Things got off to a solid enough start against the host nation. Captain David Dunn found winger Jermaine Pennant and his hard, low cross picked out Defoe, who had made an excellent run ahead of his man. There was only going to be one outcome and he poked the ball home to give England the lead. They doubled their advantage in the second half when a future strike partner of Defoe knocked in a second. Beanpole striker Peter Crouch might dwarf Defoe in the height department, but seeing both men among the goals would become a pretty familiar sight some years down the line.

Unfortunately that was as good as it got for the young Lions, as a 2-1 reverse against Italy and a 3-1 defeat by Portugal sent them crashing out in the group stages. Defoe would fail to score in either game and a disappointing summer took some of the shine off what had been a fantastic season. But despite failing to set Switzerland alight, Defoe had proved to the football community over the season that he was ready to make the step up to regular Premier League football, and maybe to senior international football as well.

Chapter 4

Frustration And Relegation

Defoe had not had his best spell in the Switzerland tournament and England's youngsters, in short, had not been good enough. But the fact remained that West Ham had re-established themselves as a Premier League force and Defoe's top-scoring season had pushed him up the pecking order. Trevor Sinclair, Joe Cole and David James had all returned from a World Cup campaign with the England senior team, while the likes of Paolo Di Canio, Frederic Kanoute and company provided additional international flair. With a boss who looked to be making strides in the right direction, the Hammers had a lot to be confident about. Moreover, during the previous campaign Glenn Roeder had made it clear more than once that young Defoe would become a more regular part of his plans. The new season was his chance to prove it.

That said, West Ham had won only three games on their travels the previous season so an opening day trip to Newcastle was never going to be easy. Things were not helped when both Di Canio and Kanoute were ruled out, meaning that while Defoe would certainly start, the 19-year-old would have to lead the line on his own. It was a position that was new to him and one that certainly did not play to his strengths. Largely isolated for the majority of the game, he never really got the kind of opportunities he thrived on and spent the game as a virtual spectator as West Ham crashed to a 4-0 defeat.

Life did not get any easier with the Hammers' first home game of the campaign – a demanding London derby against champions and double winners Arsenal. This time Defoe would have a partner up front in the returning Kanoute and West Ham's performance was a vast improvement on their opening day debacle. After Joe Cole had given them the lead, Defoe was on hand to provide a superb cross for his striking companion to put West Ham in dreamland. The dream, however, would become a nightmare as Arsenal pulled a goal back, Kanoute missed a penalty and the Gunners equalised two minutes from time. It was as though the hammering in the North East had squeezed the belief out of West Ham.

One point from a possible six made the upcoming home fixture against Charlton much more important that it should have been. While it was naturally a big game for Defoe, West Ham were already at the wrong end of the table. Early season it may have been but that is not a position anyone wants. Unfortunately, Defoe was kept well shackled by the Charlton back line, which included his childhood friend Jonathan Fortune who went on to net the winning goal. It was not ideal in a week that had seen talk growing that Defoe was worth a place in the full England squad, leading Sven-Göran Eriksson to run the rule over the striker in his team's 2-0 defeat.

While an England cap would have increased the fee West Ham had to pay Charlton for Defoe's services by a cool £250,000, Addicks boss Alan Curbishley was in no doubt over the teenager's short-term international future. 'It's too early for Defoe,' he told the media after the game. 'He needs more time to develop. He won't appreciate me saying that, but it's how I feel. We'll get more money for Jermain if he plays for England, but he'll need a full season in the Premier League before he's ready for that. You see young players being pushed for international football and huge things are expected of them.'

It would be easy to suggest that Curbishley was just being bitter. After all, he was still aggrieved by the circumstances in which Defoe quit the Valley three years previously. But his point appeared a fair one, especially when it was backed up by the teenager's own manager: 'One of my hardest jobs here is keeping a lid on all the expectations surrounding our youngsters. Things can run ahead of them and if it starts getting out of hand I'll have to step in and interfere. All the attention puts too much pressure on them and it also gives opponents more reason to go out and try to stop them.' Roeder's number one aim regarding Defoe was to protect him.

This would be made easier with the return to fitness of Paolo Di Canio. His presence in the team would again relegate the 19-year-old to the bench. Unfortunately, Di Canio's presence would also make Roeder's job of managing West Ham slightly more difficult. The manager's relationship with the Italian talisman was becoming fractious, and Defoe would become inadvertently involved. Having been replaced by Defoe in West Ham's 1-0 home defeat by newly promoted West Brom, Di Canio would unleash a verbal volley at his manager after setting up a goal in their next game, a 3-2 defeat at Spurs, before being substituted again. Roeder would not back down and brought Di Canio off for Defoe in a drab goalless draw with Manchester City at Upton Park, leaving both player and crowd somewhat irritated.

With no win in the first six games of the season and their best player at loggerheads with the manger, West Ham were struggling and so was Defoe. It looked as though the European Under-21 Championship had left him jaded and his confidence was on the wane with every disappointing Hammers result that followed. He had lost his place in the starting line-up and if his first goal of the season did not come soon he and the team would continue to suffer. So the last thing West Ham needed was a trip to Stamford Bridge.

Defoe started the game on the bench but an injury to Kanoute just four minutes into the match would give him his chance. It was the first time he and Di Canio had been paired together up front that season and he would show this was a partnership worth persevering with. After Jimmy Floyd Hasselbaink's penalty had given the Blues the lead, the two men combined as Di Canio's low corner was toe-poked in by Defoe from close range for his first goal of the season.

And what an important goal it would prove to be for West Ham. All the doubt and loss of confidence seemed to be eradicated in that one moment when Defoe's effort hit the net. The rejuvenated Hammers looked like they believed they could do anything – and when Di Canio put them in front, it looked like they really could. After collecting a loose ball some 20 yards out he flicked the ball up with his right foot before smashing it home with his left. It was a strike that left Defoe in awe as he spoke after the game: 'Paolo worked that goal entirely by himself. I'll watch it over and over again. That sort of goal isn't my style. I hang around the box and tend to get more from close range but those goals are just as important and Paolo will tell you that.'

After another Italian – future West Ham manager Gianfranco Zola – had scored a superb free-kick for Chelsea, Defoe and Di Canio combined again with six minutes to go. The young pretender put defender Mario Melchiot under pressure and the Dutchman failed to clear, allowing Di Canio to finish at the near post and earn West Ham a shock first win of the season. Defoe was delighted not only with the win, but with his first goal of the season. It had been a long time coming.

'I got 14 last year and I know I've got it in me to beat that this season, especially now the first one is out of the way,' he said after the game. 'The atmosphere in the dressing room afterwards was absolutely unbelievable. Everybody's been jumping around and going potty. It means a lot to me to score my first goal. It's always difficult to get that first one – hopefully I'll be on my way now. Glenn Roeder put me in the reserves last week so I could try and get that all-important first goal. It never came but to get one here is so special. I just can't wait until the next game now.'

As the cliché goes, goals are like London buses – you wait ages for one and then two turn up at the same time. The circumstances may have been somewhat different – a League Cup tie at Chesterfield's Saltergate – but after starting alongside Di Canio, Defoe was again on the scoresheet. He could hardly have been given an easier chance by his standards. A long ball was thumped forward by Sebastien Schemmel towards Spireites goalkeeper Carl Muggleton. Instead of coming to collect it, Muggleton stayed on his line as Defoe raced on to the loose ball and smashed it into the back of the net. It was a sweet moment of déjà vu for Defoe – Muggleton had been the Stoke goalkeeper when Defoe had scored on his debut for Bournemouth.

Muggleton had also saved a penalty that day, but he would be less fortunate this time round. While Chesterfield found an equaliser early in the second half and hung on to take the game to a penalty shoot-out, West Ham held their nerve and converted all five spot-kicks. It was a relief for the Hammers who had gone out the competition on penalties to lower-league opposition the season before.

Unfortunately for the Hammers embarrassment was to come in the next league fixture, against Premier League new boys Birmingham City at Upton Park. Having levelled the game through Joe Cole after Stern John had given the visitors the lead, West Ham threw everything they had at the visitors. Defoe himself had an excellent chance to put the Hammers in front but could only fire his shot wide. But he was not the only West Ham player that day to be wasteful in front of goal. Even the normally dependable Di Canio missed the chances that came his way as the day seemed destined to go against the home side. Their misery was compounded as John's second goal two minutes before the break proved enough to condemn West Ham to their third home defeat in five games.

It looked as though both Defoe and West Ham were becoming more effective when they were away from Upton Park, a bizarre statistic when the previous season their home record had been matched only by champions Arsenal. After Trevor Sinclair had given the Hammers the lead at Sunderland, Defoe very nearly set the Stadium of Light alight with a scintillating run that left the Wearsiders' defence floundering in his wake. He managed to pick out Joe Cole

Defoe lines up for the
England U18s in 2001.

Above: Defoe celebrates scoring on his debut for the England U21 side against Mexico in 2001.

Below: With England and future Tottenham team-mate Peter Crouch at the England training camp, preparing for the 2002 U21 European Championships.

Defoe with the rest of the England U21 side (*above*) and in action at the 2002 U21 European Championships. Unfortunately England finished bottom of their group but during his U21 career Defoe made 23 appearances and scored seven goals.

Defoe in action for West Ham. He turned professional with the club aged 16 and finished as top scorer in 2001/2, but relegation the following season was instrumental in his move to Spurs.

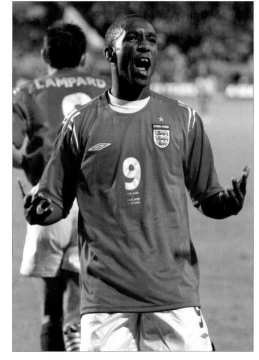

Above: Defoe rues a missed chance on his full England debut against Sweden in March 2004.

Below left and right: Helping England qualify for the 2006 World Cup. Despite impressing in qualification, Defoe was left out of the squad for the finals in Germany.

Defoe in action for Tottenham Hotspur. He signed for the club in 2004 and enjoyed a magnificent first season, being named Player of the Year.

Above: Squaring up to referee Mike Dean in a Carling Cup match against Bolton Wanderers.

Below: Defoe (*back row, second from right*) with the rest of the England squad before a friendly against Denmark in 2005.

Above: Defoe gets stuck in against Grimsby Town.

Below: Visiting Wembley during construction of the new stadium in 2005.

but the England player's effort was brilliantly saved by the Sunderland keeper. Sinclair's strike proved to be the winner as West Ham conjured up only their second league win of the season. But Defoe had still only scored twice and if the Hammers were going to get themselves out of the relegation dogfight, then he – and those around him – would need to do more.

They would get the opportunity at Loftus Road. Queen's Park Rangers' home ground was a temporary home for Fulham while their Craven Cottage ground was being upgraded and it was proving to be a happy hunting ground for them. But as on their previous visit to west London, the Hammers would end another unbeaten run. Again Defoe would not score, but again his all-round contribution was first class, again in front of a watching representative of the England team, this time Mr Eriksson's assistant, Tord Grip. Early in the game Defoe saw what looked a perfectly legitimate goal ruled out for offside, then he was denied by keeper Edwin van der Sar in a one-on-one. But such was Defoe's desire to help the cause he powered into the area and forced defender Zat Knight into a clumsy, late challenge to earn a penalty, which Di Canio duly converted. Defoe had helped the Hammers to their second straight win.

But just as the green shoots of recovery looked to be sprouting in West Ham's faltering season, they were cut short by two defeats in a row against the Merseyside clubs. Defoe's bad luck in front of goal continued in a home game against Everton, whose goalkeeper Richard Wright was in sparkling form to keep out the striker's deflected effort in a one-goal defeat. Defoe also failed to find the net in West Ham's 2-0 defeat at the hands of Liverpool, but his perceived value to the team was demonstrated in the 66th minute when he was substituted. Glenn Roeder's decision to remove the youngster from the fray was met with a furious reaction from the travelling fans. They had paid their money to make the long trip to Anfield with the hope of seeing the team make the best attempt possible at picking up an unlikely win. And the only way to do that, in their opinion, was with Defoe in the team.

The youngster was clearly frustrated. The team was not winning and he was not scoring. His angst was plain to see as West Ham crashed out of the League Cup in a humiliating home defeat by Oldham. He wasted two good opportunities to score and his partnership with new signing Titi Camara failed to click. To rub salt in the wound, he was booked in the second half for diving after a fall that was theatrical to say the least. At the final whistle the Hammers fans were furious and let the team know in no uncertain terms.

The Hammers were now in serious trouble. Turfed out of the League Cup by a Division Two team, struggling near the foot of the Premier League table, without a win at home all season and now the fans were starting to turn on the manager and his players. The home form did not look like improving any time soon either, with Leeds and Manchester United the visitors to Upton Park in the next two games.

The Leeds game was dismal. Defoe missed a great chance with a mistimed header that drifted harmlessly wide as the hosts found themselves 4-1 down and out of the game by half-time. They managed to pull two back in the second half but it was too little too late. It was the perfect encapsulation of their inconsistent ways. With the likes of Di Canio partnering Defoe up front, and further precocious young talents in Joe Cole and Michael Carrick alongside them, there was no doubting the quality they had. The problem was getting them all to fire at the same time.

By the time the Manchester United game came round, not many people gave West Ham a chance. As usual, the Red Devils were going for the Premier League title and were strong favourites to beat a team who hadn't won at home all season. Surely there could be only one winner. Again Sven-Göran Eriksson was in town, but he was there to run the rule over such names as Paul Scholes, David James and Joe Cole. Jermain Defoe was struggling for form, struggling for goals and had all but proved he was nowhere near ready for a call-up to the full England squad. Fortunately, there seemed to be one person who had not been told – someone who had scored two goals in his last two games against the Premier League heavyweights. That person was Jermain Defoe.

It was no surprise when Manchester United took the lead seven minutes before half-time through Ruud van Nistelrooy, although there were some serious suspicions of offside. United created plenty of chances but could not find a way past James, who was in inspired form. But the home side came out after the break displaying a resilience and fight that belied their position at the bottom of the table. Both Defoe and Cole hit the woodwork as West Ham refused to lie down and die as they had done after going behind against Leeds. This West Ham side was determined to put on the kind of show that their fans had been waiting for all season. They had impressed against Arsenal and beaten Chelsea. Why should they not spring a surprise against Manchester United?

Four minutes from time it happened. Defoe, who also appeared offside, poked the ball beyond keeper Fabien Barthez to send the home fans into delirium. He had made it three goals in three games against Manchester United – the kind of record that some of the finest players in world football would be delighted with. By the time the final whistle came, West Ham had still not managed to win at home, but they had shown enough to give their fans hope that they would not be rooted at the bottom of the table for much longer.

A delighted Glenn Roeder was in no doubt as to who deserved the most praise, with his youngest forward drawing the plaudits for hard work that had finally got the reward it deserved. 'This will be the toughest period in his footballing life,' Roeder said, 'because we are having to play him as the main striker up through the middle. I am sure that one day when he plays as the second striker – which he really is – and he has someone with a bigger physical presence alongside him it will help him. If Freddie Kanoute had been fit, I would have rested him a few games ago but I've had to keep playing him when it's been tough. He's only just 20 and he's stayed with it when things haven't been going his way and worked hard for the team. If anyone deserved to score that goal it was him.'

West Ham were still without a win in five games but the draw had arrested their barren run of four straight defeats. However, there had already been false dawns, even though the season was not yet at its halfway point. This impressive result would mean nothing if the Hammers could not capitalise on it. They had now impressed against three of the bigger teams in the Premier League, but if they could not back it up with positive results against the rest, they would be in trouble regardless of how well they performed.

That point was proven when West Ham travelled to the Midlands to face fellow strugglers Aston Villa. Defoe was at the heart of the visitors' bright opening to the game when he shot inches wide after a display of individual skill and trickery that had left experienced campaigner Steve Staunton tied up in knots. Defoe then had an effort disallowed for offside, but seconds later Villa took the lead. The hosts never looked back as they dominated the game from then on. Di Canio scored a consolation goal for West Ham but a final score of 4-1 condemned them to the bottom of the Premier League table. The run of games without a win was getting longer and longer, and for all the plaudits he had received, Defoe had still only scored three goals all season, only two of which had come in the league.

His struggles would continue against Southampton, as would West Ham's woeful form on their own turf. Defoe failed to connect with one effort after sublime work from Di Canio and saw his mistimed shot bobble wide, then he snatched at another good opportunity late on. It was clear to see that his confidence was low. The past two years had seen him scoring goals for fun: he was not used to the chances not hitting the back of the net. His misery was confirmed in injury time when James Beattie made it six home defeats in nine games for the Hammers.

There was more late drama against Middlesbrough at the Riverside which ultimately cost West Ham victory. A loose shot from Defoe was thumped in by Ian Pearce to give the visitors a 2-1 lead but Ugo Ehiogu rescued a point for Boro that kept the Hammers rock bottom. Their cause was not helped the following week as they travelled to Old Trafford in mid-December and suffered a 3-0 defeat.

Defoe had a goal disallowed for offside and as a result his fine run against Manchester United came to an end. He also had a strong shout for a penalty turned down very early in the game after being sent tumbling by Phil Neville. Television replays indicated that Defoe had been hard done by in both incidents. It is often said in football that luck never goes the way of a team that is struggling, and West Ham were looking like the perfect example of that. It was turning into a real winter of discontent for West Ham.

Defoe missed more chances in the relegation six-pointer against Bolton at Upton Park, which ended in a 1-1 draw. Despite setting up the opening goal for temporary strike partner Pearce, he missed a header from close range and was denied on several occasions by Trotters keeper Jussi Jaaskelainen. Worse, the writing seemed to be on the wall when Roeder spoke after the game of his need to have Frederic Kanoute back in the team and fully fit. He also wanted to bring another striker to the club in the January transfer window to cure what he saw as the problem: 'We are creating far too many chances for the few we are scoring.'

The team followed this 1-1 draw with another at home to Fulham. Kanoute's return to the team did not bring the goals that Roeder was after, though Defoe was the man to go closest when he saw a free-kick crash back off the post. However, his performance was not enough to keep him in the team for the trip to Blackburn. He had been the one to suffer from West Ham's dreadful home form, which saw them end 2002 without a single win at Upton Park in the first half of the season.

Defoe's relegation back to the bench was obviously not ideal for him but it seemed to benefit West Ham – whenever he came off the bench he scored a crucial late goal. The draw at Ewood Park was no exception. With just four minutes left and the Hammers heading for another defeat, he emerged from the sidelines to pounce on a loose ball in the box to grab a hugely important point for his team. It prompted more praise from the manager, but once again it was tempered by reality. 'Everyone knows we are short on the striking department,' Roeder said. 'Losing Freddie Kanoute and Paolo Di Canio has really wounded us. That's not a criticism of young Defoe. He's battled manfully over the last few months, but he's only a kid. With his lack of physical presence he needs that bigger person alongside him.'

Defoe would be back in the starting line-up at the turn of the year as West Ham began 2003 with something they had been striving for since August – a home win. Admittedly it came in the FA Cup against opposition a division below in Nottingham Forest, but Defoe's double lifted some of the gloom around the East End. His first goal was a thing of beauty, as he cut inside from the left-hand edge of the penalty area to curl in a sumptuous right-footed effort. With seven minutes left he scored another late winner as a bobbling strike took a fortuitous deflection on its way into the bottom corner.

Defoe's confidence looked to be back. He had scored three times in his last two games and he continued in the same vein in the next match. Unfortunately, West Ham's home form in the league would not improve. A late equaliser from Jermaine Jenas cancelled out Defoe's opener on the stroke of half-time to leave the Hammers still searching for that elusive home league victory. For Defoe, it was another lovely goal as he turned defender Steve Caldwell before rifling his shot into the bottom corner. For all that his manager wanted to give Defoe a rest, it was looking like Roeder had to play him if his team were to stay up. He would score again at Highbury against Arsenal – his most impressive run in the claret and blue of West Ham – but a 3-1 defeat did little to boost team morale.

The results would only get worse, and with them the

striker's confidence in front of goal would ebb away. The home crowd at the Valley would always make things difficult for Defoe regardless of how his team was performing, but West Ham's current plight gave the young man very little to work with as Charlton cruised to a comfortable 4-2 victory. Again he squandered an excellent opportunity to keep his team in the game but goalkeeper Dean Kiely made a block that seemed to sum up the forward's season up – he was still getting into the right positions to score but he was not finding the net with enough regularity. Yes, he had scored in four consecutive games, but after ten in a row for Bournemouth he was now judging himself – and others were judging him – on different criteria. Every game without a goal appeared like another step in the direction of impending doom for West Ham – a notion not helped by a 6-0 drubbing by Manchester United in the next round of the FA Cup. Could anything stop the rot?

Defoe was back among the substitutes for the next home fixture against Blackburn. It was not long since he'd stolen a point against them from the bench, so Roeder must have been hopeful that lightning would strike twice. Di Canio was back in the team, alongside January signing Les Ferdinand – the experienced campaigner and Premier League legend who could provide the physical presence the manager had desperately wanted. But even the two big names up front could not change the 1-1 scoreline by the time Defoe eventually took to the field in the 84th minute. The youngster, however, could.

He picked the ball up on the left before controlling it and moving towards goal. With the speed of touch he was becoming known for, he unleashed a low shot that zipped between two Blackburn defenders and into the net. Lightning had indeed struck twice. Finally, *finally*, West Ham had won a Premier League game at home.

But typically, *typically*, they followed it up with a home defeat. Despite his heroics in midweek, Defoe was kept on the bench until Liverpool had sewn up all three points at Upton Park. He was given just as little chance to impress in the trip to Leeds that followed, as West Ham lost again and stayed in the bottom three.

He was given more of an opportunity against West Brom at the Hawthorns, but again he would fail to score. However, that was not the whole story as his introduction sparked another confrontation between the manager and Paolo Di Canio, who, while clearly unfit, was in no mood to give up his place in the side to anybody. It proved of little consequence, however, as West Ham got back to winning ways with a 2-1 victory. Perhaps things were starting to look up.

That was certainly how things seemed after a second home win of the season, against Tottenham. Defoe was paired up front with Les Ferdinand for the first time and the partnership seemed to work immediately – as Roeder had predicted. The powerful Ferdinand was the perfect foil for Defoe's small and speedy presence. The younger of the two was inspirational, chasing every loose ball, causing defenders no end of trouble and nearly getting a goal, had it not been for a fine save by Kasey Keller. But when the goal did come, it was almost entirely Defoe's doing. His dazzling flick took two Spurs defenders out of the equation before he squared to his new partner, and Ferdinand made no mistake from close range. Michael Carrick rounded off the scoring as West Ham achieved a crucial win.

A draw at Everton was followed by another home win as the Hammers' survival fight finally clicked into gear. Sunderland were the visitors this time and Defoe would be the man to set them on their way. Again he combined with Ferdinand, the old warhorse returning the favour from the Spurs game with a deft header to his youthful partner, whose shot on the turn was unstoppable. As West Ham moved out of the relegation zone for the first time in 20 games, Roeder was in no doubt about the success of the new duo. He told the media: 'Defoe worked his socks off and now he is learning a lot in training from Les Ferdinand, who he has the utmost respect for. Defoe is a quick learner and he's now picking up things without me having to tell him. He has the gift to score goals and ever since I saw him as a 16-year-old at Lilleshall he has had that twinkle in his eye. He has that belief that strikers need to have. He has become a better all-round player and he has become important to our aim.'

Defoe's performance, in front of the England coach, left onlookers enthusing about his prospects. Here he was, in a team that looked increasingly likely for the drop, still putting in the kind of performances and scoring the kind of goals that would be expected in a team at the right end of the table. His late equaliser against Southampton would prove to be his final goal of the season, leaving his total at 11, but it stretched his team's unbeaten run to six games. Roeder was again effusive in his praise: 'He's learned so much throughout what has been a tough season for us and his mental strength and belief is incredible for a 20-year-old. He always believes he is going to score – he got one good chance, and he finished it easily.'

He did miss a great chance for another goal – as he did in West Ham's next game at home to Aston Villa, which finished

2-2 – but it spoke volumes about the young man's ability when Villa and former England manager Graham Taylor proclaimed: 'When a forward like Defoe is through, you expect him to put the ball in the net.'

But put the ball in the net you must do, and despite his impressive form, Defoe would discover how fine the line was between success and failure at the highest level. A few days after the Villa game he was nominated for the Professional Football Association Young Player of the Year award – but then missed chance after chance after chance as West Ham crashed to their first defeat in seven games at the hands of relegation rivals Bolton at the Reebok. It was a bad-tempered affair that ended in an ugly brawl – the clearest indication yet that the Hammers' frustrations were finally getting the better of them. Despite returning home to win against Middlesbrough, they were dealt another cruel blow.

In the aftermath of the game, Glenn Roeder collapsed at the ground. It transpired he had suffered a blockage to a blood vessel in his brain. Roeder would return to the dugout, but not before the end of the season. It was a terrible piece of news that seemed to put all of West Ham's footballing troubles into perspective. However, the fact remained it was another blow to a team that had finally looked to be making progress. Hammers legend Trevor Brooking took charge of the team for the remainder of the campaign.

If anything, the tragic news seemed to galvanise the team. They went on to pick up back-to-back wins at Manchester City and at home to Chelsea – the latter game an emotional affair as Paolo Di Canio scored the winner on what was to be his last game at Upton Park in West Ham colours. But it was all too little too late come the final day of the season. The

Hammers' 2-2 draw at Birmingham was immaterial as Bolton won their final game, condemning them to relegation with 42 points – the highest total ever achieved by a relegated side. Their stirring end to the season had not proved enough. And with relegation came a stark realisation for Jermain Defoe: staying at Upton Park would deprive him of the top-level football he so wanted to play.

That realisation would lead Defoe to make one of the most controversial decisions of his career. The day after West Ham were relegated from the Premier League he handed in a written transfer request. His reasons for leaving appeared similar to his reason for choosing the Hammers over Charlton when he'd first turned professional. 'This is very much a career decision,' he said at the time. 'I am very ambitious and hungry to achieve at the highest levels of the game for both club and country.' His intentions seemed fair enough. After all, he had always made clear that he was keen to reach the very top of the game as quickly as possible. In addition, his ability had not gone unnoticed by the national team management and he knew that to make the step up from under-21 to senior international football he would need to be playing in the top flight.

However, the timing of the event was not the best. He received criticism from all quarters, including his own team-mates. Goalkeeper David James, himself an England international, was one of the first to question his companion's judgement. He told *The Times*: 'Everyone knows the club will have to make changes to cope with our reduced circumstances. But the right thing to do is let the club work out where it stands first. I can only hope that Jermain Defoe was acting on the advice of someone else when he submitted a written transfer request. We have not even been relegated for 48 hours, so I do not think it is helpful, even if he thinks it is best for his career.'

As it transpired, Defoe had acted on the advice of his management. West Ham's managing director Paul Aldridge confirmed that the club had refused the transfer request and that they were trying to work with Defoe to reach a compromise. In an interview with the club's official website he said: 'Jermain is a smashing lad from a good family. We have a good relationship with him and them, and it is unfortunate that he has received advice to put in a request at this time. That advice has led to criticism from supporters and work colleagues alike. I would, however, caution our supporters to be patient with Jermain.'

Defoe would eventually apologise to the supporters, but it was always going to be difficult for them to support a man who had grown up with their club before deciding he did not want to stick with them through their darkest hour. While it was easy to understand the professional reasons for Defoe's desire to move on, the West Ham fans would forever struggle to accept the personal reasons for not wanting to help them return to the Premier League and continue his quest for top-level football with them. However, if Defoe's early season form was anything to go by, the Hammers fans would probably be happy enough to hang on to Defoe for as long as possible, whether he wanted to be there or not.

The manager was certainly happy to have Defoe on board. While it was evident Roeder would have preferred his star striker to have kept quiet while he was still in hospital, his return to work would have been helped by the knowledge that Defoe was still at the club as West Ham looked to recover from the previous season's problems. The competition for places that had existed before had all but gone, with Di Canio, Kanoute and Joe Cole all having moved on, so Defoe was now the ace in the pack.

Despite mounting speculation about an approach from the Premier League, that's the way it was on the opening day of the 2003/04 season, when a close-range equaliser sent his team on their way to a 2-1 win at Preston North End. His reputation had preceded him as he came into second-tier football for the first time, with Preston manager Craig Brown saying afterwards: 'I just wish someone had signed Defoe before today – he's a very good player.' The Hammers faithful would see first hand what Brown was talking about in the first home game of the season, a League Cup first-round victory against Rushden & Diamonds, when he was on hand to put away the rebound from a shot off the crossbar.

However, more change was afoot at Upton Park. Following a defeat at Rotherham soon afterwards, the West Ham board decided to part company with Glenn Roeder and again appointed Trevor Brooking in a caretaker capacity. His first game back in charge would be at home against Bradford, when Defoe would make it a happy homecoming with the only goal of the game – and what a goal. A dazzling run took him past three bewildered Bradford defenders before he let fly with wonderful shot that flew past Bantams keeper Mark Paston into the corner of the net.

Defoe grabbed his fourth goal in six games at Portman Road as West Ham saw off Ipswich 2-1, and it was almost as stunning as his solo effort that sunk Bradford. Again he would show his fleet-footedness to devastating effect as he beat two defenders on the right and cut inside to hammer a 20-yard shot into the net. He was going through a purple patch in front of goal, but there was another side to his game that was going to prove a problem.

While on loan at Bournemouth and early in his West Ham career, there had been flashes of petulance from Defoe. Only flashes, mind – the odd angry word here, an exaggerated fall there, a rash challenge or two. But as he approached his 21st birthday, it was becoming apparent that the frustration of not being allowed to leave and play at the highest level was starting to get to him. As West Ham crumbled to a 2-0 defeat at Gillingham, Defoe said something abusive enough to linesman Mark Ives to warrant a straight red card. It was a foolish act but one that was born out of annoyance rather than any ill feeling or bad nature.

But before serving his ban, he would show the positive side of his game with four goals in his next three matches, starting with a trip to Cardiff in the second round of the League Cup. The Bluebirds raced into a two-goal lead but then Defoe took over. After pulling a goal back from the penalty spot following a foul on strike partner David Connolly, he then levelled the scores with a deflected effort midway through the second half. Finally, in the last minute of normal time, he struck home a superb effort from the edge of the penalty area to claim his first ever hat-trick at senior level.

Despite failing to score in the next game against Millwall, he lit up the final game before his suspension with a lovely goal in a 3-0 win in another London derby, this time at home to Crystal Palace. When the Eagles' Michael Hughes under-hit a backpass to his goalkeeper Cedric Berthelin, Defoe nipped in to execute a magnificent dummy and take the ball round the French custodian before rolling it into an empty net.

Defoe's second game back after his ban was new manager Alan Pardew's first in charge. If the former Reading boss had any doubts about what Defoe could do, they were soon laid to rest with a textbook header from Matthew Etherington's cross to seal a point at home against Nottingham Forest. It was only October and the 21-year-old was already just one goal shy of double figures.

He would have to wait until November to reach that milestone before going on yet another mini-spree. But again questions would be asked about his temperament. After giving the Hammers the lead in a 1-1 draw at Coventry City with a smart run and finish, he opened the scoring in the first minute at home to West Brom. However, after racing into a 3-0 lead, the Hammers managed to lose 4-3, thanks partly to a clumsy and needless challenge on Sean Gregan from Defoe which earned him a red card. Pardew stopped short of blaming Defoe, but conceded that the incident had cost his team. 'I think Jermain can count himself very unlucky to be sent off,' said the manager. 'It was just exuberance on his part. But it did change the game and it will be another massive blow to lose him through suspension.' Defoe would miss the next five games.

As if to underline just how what the Hammers had missed, Defoe scored two more in his next game, at home to Sunderland. The first was a tap-in after keeper Mart Poom had spilled a cross, the second a tidy finish from Etherington's pullback as West Ham again came from two goals behind to win a match. Defoe was finding the back of the net with remarkable ease at this level and as January edged closer it was little surprise to see speculation about his future increasing.

Unfortunately as one suspension ended, another was on the horizon. He was deemed to have aimed a kick at Walsall's Ian

Roper in a 1-1 draw at the Bescot Stadium – an unhappy return to the ground where he'd made his first-team debut – as his frustration again got the better of him. Roper thought that the sending off was harsh, but Defoe was given his marching orders for the third time in the season.

As things turned out, he would only play two more games for West Ham, but not surprisingly he would score in both of them. After having his appeals for a penalty waved away before skewing an excellent chance wide against Ipswich at Upton Park, he gave his side the lead when he diverted home Marlon Harewood's cross. It was not enough, however, as West Ham lost the game 2-1. But he made sure to sign off with a bang in his final game for the Hammers.

Harewood had given West Ham the lead against Nottingham Forest at the City Ground early on, but the travelling fans would have to wait until six minutes from time to see their soon-to-depart favourite's swansong goal. A long ball from centre-back Tomas Repka put the home defence under pressure, allowing Defoe to race on to the ball and hammer home his last goal in claret and blue. It was his 15th goal of the season, meaning he had already topped his previous season's best for the club in just half a season. In total he had scored 41 goals in his 105 appearances.

As 2003 came to a close, the only question that remained was where Defoe was going to play his football. Many in the media had linked him to Premier League champions Manchester United and also to Chelsea. However, there was one man who felt that the striker was still not ready for a move to one of the bigger clubs.

After Glenn Roeder had left West Ham, Defoe had claimed in the press that he could have helped save the Hammers from relegation if he had been given more playing time. It was a claim that Roeder refuted vigorously. 'He started 29 league games of our Premiership season. He was on the bench for the other nine games and the majority of those he got on the field of play. In those 38 games he scored eight goals which, for a player with his reputation, is disappointing. I set him a target at the start of the season for what was expected of him and he didn't get near that.'

Roeder went on to criticise Defoe for the sendings-off he had received in the early part of the season and suggested that no big club wanted to take a gamble on him. He added: 'I don't know if he thinks I stopped him leaving in the summer. But the fact is this: if anyone had come in for him before the club raised the money it needed, he would have been sold. But nobody did. They came in for Glen Johnson, Trevor Sinclair, Freddie Kanoute and Joe Cole and that raised the money. I think Jermain's still finding it difficult to come to terms with the fact no one came in for him. It's time to get over it.'

But in this January transfer window, somebody would come in for Jermain Defoe. It was to be one of the Premier League's bigger clubs, with the aim of giving him the chance to play regular top flight football, with the added bonus of enhancing his prospects of getting into the senior national team. Regardless of the comments made by Roeder, regardless of how Defoe felt he had been treated at West Ham and regardless of whether he should have made his ill-timed transfer request, he would finally be given the opportunity he so desperately craved – the chance to score goals in the Premier League again.

Chapter 5

Earning His Spurs

How ironic that it should be Tottenham Hotspur who answered the call. Defoe had grown up an Arsenal supporter and he had developed as a player at West Ham United. If fans of either club could choose one team to avoid for the rest of their days it would probably be the one from White Hart Lane. But here they were, offering Defoe the opportunity to lead their attacking line for the remainder of the 2003/04 season and beyond. Not only that, Spurs would reunite Defoe with his old Hammers strike partner Freddie Kanoute, who had already been a success story since his move to north London.

Defoe's transfer came about as part of a cash plus player deal that cost Tottenham a total of £7 million plus striker Bobby Zamora, who had disappointed since moving to the Lane. West Ham had been pretty much resigned to losing Defoe at some point after the transfer request fiasco, and manager Alan

Pardew was honest enough with his assessment of the move. 'It's always difficult to lose a great player,' he said, 'but in the cold light of day we knew all the facts, and the fact is he wouldn't sign a new contract with us. I rang him on Sunday night and got a feel for where he was at, and that made my decision. On numerous occasions he had been asked to come in and he made it very clear – well, not so much him but his agency – made it clear they were not prepared to do a deal.'

In his comments about Zamora, Pardew said how happy he was to have a player who showed he wanted to play for the club. Perhaps a thinly veiled dig at his outgoing star? It was certainly a sentiment echoed by Pete May, author of the West Ham book *Irons in the Soul*, who said, 'Defoe's attitude did not endear him to West Ham fans at all. Alan Pardew had no choice but to get players in who want to play for the club.' Hammers fans were quick to join in as online message boards were filled with comments suggesting Defoe's disciplinary problems on the pitch were purely the result of his desire to get away from Upton Park. Perhaps it was an understandable criticism – after all, two five-game bans had ensured that Defoe only played 22 out of 34 possible games at the start of the season before his move.

It seemed as though all the coverage surrounding Defoe's move across London was focused on his attitude. People were quick to point out that the advice he took from his management company, SFX, indicated a lack of mental strength that would cost him a place with one of the biggest clubs in the Premier League. Commentators made mention of the fact that instead of Defoe, Manchester United and Arsenal had signed Louis Saha and Jose Antonio Reyes respectively in that transfer window, citing Defoe's mentality as a reason. It was as though people in the game had taken as gospel the words of West Ham chairman Terence Brown when he said Defoe's 'head wasn't right' when he put in his transfer request, a comment that upset the youngster.

'His comments were a shock and they hurt me,' said Defoe. 'To have something like that said about you is not nice. But I had my family around me as well as my agent and they all told me just to get on with my football and let that do the talking.' It is the only way to respond as a footballer when people are determined to focus on everything but your football.

In fact Defoe came to recognise that the manner in which he had handed in his transfer request was far from ideal. The club had just been relegated and the manager was seriously ill in hospital. There was no real way to justify the timing of the move when the circumstances were taken into consideration. Defoe realised this and addressed the matter after being unveiled at White Hart Lane. 'I mishandled that move and I can only apologise,' he told journalists. 'I'm young and I have learned from it. I still played my hardest for West Ham and gave them 100 per cent and want to thank the fans for their support. They've been great to me ever since I came through as a 17-year-old.' Football fans rarely forgive a perceived betrayal, but 15 goals in half a season suggested Defoe had still tried up to his very last game in claret and blue.

With so many questions being asked about his attitude and mentality and everything else that was wrong with Defoe, people seemed to be forgetting what was right with him. But one man who was quick to praise him was the man who had convinced the Spurs boardroom to part company with a lot of money for a player who had yet to convince everybody of his talent. Acting manager David Pleat could not wait to see his newest star in action and made it clear that his own aims matched the ambitions of Defoe. 'I can't think of a British striker at his age who has achieved as much in such a short space of time,' he said. 'His goal record for a 21-year-old is quite exceptional. I hope he will have a fine career at Tottenham. This keeps our policy of wanting to develop a young team with prospects to really improve and get into Europe.'

Defoe's job would not be easy. While he admitted he was looking forward to teaming up with his old pal Kanoute again, Spurs had plenty of other striking talent in the form of fans' favourite Robbie Keane and young Portuguese international Helder Postiga. This was not a situation that was alien to Defoe, but it would be a real challenge to earn a place in the starting line-up. However, after his debut in February, he would prove himself to be a valuable addition to the Tottenham team. Not only that, but the biggest dream of all was about to come true.

In his short career, Defoe had made a habit of scoring goals on his debut. He had done it for West Ham, for Bournemouth and for England under-21s. So when the opportunity came his way at White Hart Lane against Portsmouth, the home crowd were waiting for their newest hero to do what had made him so famous so soon. They had to wait just 13 minutes for a wonderfully taken strike to justify all that expectation. Peeling away from his man, he received the ball from Keane and hammered his shot low and hard through the legs of a defender and across his former West Ham team-mate Shaka Hislop. It was the perfect start to the latest chapter in his career, made even sweeter by Gus Poyet's last-gasp winner to clinch a 4-3 win.

Things would get even better for Defoe when he made another return to Charlton Athletic. As usual, his every touch would be booed and jeered by the Valley faithful who had still not forgotten his history with the club – a taste of what was to come when he would eventually return to Upton Park to face West Ham. After his frustrating previous visit to his old home, Defoe laid his demons to rest with Spurs' second goal in a 4-2 victory. As his venomous shot ricocheted into the net off goalkeeper Dean Kiely, he unleashed a roar of delight. He had faced enough critics in the last month and that goal would go some way to silencing some of them.

However, the two positive results in Defoe's opening Tottenham exchanges did little to alter the erratic form that had plagued the club all season. Despite scoring twice at White Hart Lane against Leicester, Spurs threw away a 3-1 lead to draw 4-4. With 12 goals in three games it was clear the team had plenty to offer going forward, but defensive frailties were costing them dear. Even Defoe was feeling the pain, despite scoring four times in his first three. 'I'm devastated, we should have won the game,' he told the media after the game. 'It's really disappointing but it helps to have great players around me.'

He would soon have even more great players around him, but not at White Hart Lane. Defoe's next six games for the club would pass without him finding the back of the net, and even more worryingly with five defeats and only one win. However, during that time Defoe would get the news he was desperate to hear – the news that he had been waiting for since the very start of his career, that maybe, privately, he had been expecting one day to hear.

England were due to head to Portugal in the summer of

2004 for the European Championships and had arranged a friendly game against Sweden in Gothenburg in late March as part of their preparation. With Michael Owen injured (although surely on the plane for the finals), there was a place open for the Scandinavian friendly. And with seven goals in 23 England Under-21 games, 19 goals this season already and a further 25 Premier League goals in two seasons with West Ham, that place went to Defoe. Finally, he would have the chance to prove himself at international level.

The newest member of the England party would not start the game in Sweden's second city as Everton's Wayne Rooney and another former under-21 star Darius Vassell took the field. But Defoe would get a taste of the action a lot sooner than he expected. Vassell went down with an ankle injury following a heavy challenge from his Aston Villa club-mate Olof Mellberg and was forced to leave the field. Instead of turning to his more experienced strikers Alan Smith and Emile Heskey, Sven-Göran Eriksson gave the nod to Defoe.

It nearly paid off immediately. Almost straight after entering the field of play, Defoe found space in the box to flash a shot across the face of goal. Rooney managed to divert the ball towards the net but it struck the post and rebounded agonisingly away. It was the start of what was to be an inspired contribution by Defoe, whose partnership with Rooney looked to have clicked from the off. A skilful flick from the teenage Evertonian allowed Defoe to use his pace to shrug off Mellberg and power a shot into the legs of goalkeeper Andreas Isaksson, this after he had nearly stunned the Ullevi Stadium with a bicycle kick that shook the side netting. He would go close again in the second half with a run and shot that was tipped over the bar by substitute keeper Magnus Kihlstedt.

Unfortunately for Defoe and England, a single goal by Zlatan Ibrahimovic would be enough to clinch the win for Sweden, but there was little doubt about who England's star performer had been. Even Sven was impressed, telling BBC Radio 5 Live: 'Jermain did very well – I liked what I saw. He showed that he can do very well even in international football and that he is technically very good. Jermain is quick and he knows where the goal is, so I like him very much.'

But would that be enough to earn Defoe a place at Euro 2004? The new kid on the block was certainly optimistic but diplomatic. 'I'll leave that to Mr Eriksson to decide,' Defoe said. 'Now I just need to go back to my club, work hard and keep my feet on the ground. It was a dream come true to play at senior level and I really enjoyed it.'

Defoe would only score three more goals on his return to club action as Tottenham stuttered to a final Premier League position of 14th. The first came in a drab 1-1 draw with Manchester City as he turned his man and fired under former West Ham colleague David James. He then netted the winner against Blackburn at the Lane to end a barren run of eight games without a victory. It was an important moment for Defoe, whose impressive left-footed volley was seen by England assistant coach Tord Grip.

But despite ending the season in style with the second goal in a 2-0 win at Wolves, there would be disappointment for Defoe. Despite featuring briefly in a friendly tournament against Japan and Iceland in June, he was left out of the final England party for Portugal. However, there were a number of reasons to be cheerful. He was playing in the Premier League again, he was at a club that had genuine ambition to progress and he had finally made the step up to senior international football. The future was looking bright as 2004/05 approached.

As the new season began a fresh optimism surrounded White Hart Lane. The fans had been given the change in management that they were looking for, with David Pleat making way for Frenchman Jacques Santini, who would be backed up by Dutch coach and former West Brom and Coventry player Martin Jol. The squad had been strengthened in some key areas, but the new management had faith in the strikers already at the club. Defoe in particular would be used regularly as Tottenham set about improving on last season's mid-table finish.

Spurs got the opportunity to show how far they intended to progress on the opening day of the season. They faced a home game against Liverpool, who had full expectations themselves of playing against Europe's elite. It was an interesting match-up between two managers who had come from abroad to improve the fortunes of their new clubs, with Santini at Tottenham and Spaniard Rafael Benitez now in charge at Anfield. It was just a shame that, as a spectacle, the quality of the game could not match the anticipation and intrigue surrounding it, as the two teams played out a somewhat dreary 1-1 draw.

There was, however, one livewire performance and it came from Defoe. After Premier League new boy Djibril Cisse had fired Liverpool into the lead, it was left to England's latest striking hope to haul his team back into the game. He nearly did so with the most skilful moment of the match, when one swift movement accounted for two Reds defenders before a delightful chip dropped just wide of the far post. But it did not take long for Defoe to adjust his radar as he expertly controlled Kanoute's flick-on and struck home the equaliser. He could have won the game late on with a snap shot that just missed the target, but it did little to detract from what had been another solid performance, again in front of Sven-Göran Eriksson. 'It's always nice to score when the England manager is in the crowd,' smiled Defoe afterwards.

Regardless of Mr Eriksson's thoughts, the new Spurs boss was impressed by his first viewing of the 21-year-old and hinted at big things to come. 'Jermain did very well for us and it was a great goal,' said Santini in his post-match press conference. 'It is far too early in the season to say whether he will be a Golden Boot contender but he has many qualities as a striker.' As a former France manager who had worked with the likes of Thierry Henry and David Trezeguet, Santini knew a good striker when he saw one. It was the perfect boost for Defoe as he looked to push his career on to the next level.

Eriksson had clearly been impressed too as he called up Defoe for England's first game of the season, a home friendly against Ukraine to prepare for the upcoming 2006 World Cup qualification double-header against Austria and Poland. The striker would only play 45 minutes, coming on as a half-time substitute for Alan Smith, but although he did not get on the scoresheet, he produced another lively showing to fashion two chances to score. The first was a scrambled effort that drifted wide, and the second a shot that was well saved by the Ukrainian goalkeeper. However, the missed opportunities would not dampen his spirits. Again he had performed well in an England shirt, and this time the national team were victorious as they went on to claim a comfortable 3-0 win.

Defoe was on the crest of a wave. Despite not scoring in Spurs' next game, an impressive 1-0 win at Newcastle, he would be back doing exactly what he did best in the two games that followed. Although Tottenham fell a goal behind early at the Hawthorns against West Brom, they dominated the game thereafter and got their just rewards with the equalising goal courtesy of Defoe's right foot. Once again he would combine effectively with his old friend Kanoute and his 25-yard thunderbolt zipped beyond the Baggies goalkeeper. Once again he would have chances to guarantee all three points that he did not take, but Santini remained happy enough. 'I hope he can continue playing like that,' he commented.

He certainly could keep playing like that, and again he would score at White Hart Lane with Sven-Göran Eriksson watching. The Swede got another reminder that Defoe was looking like the perfect pick as England prepared to travel to Central Europe in search of crucial World Cup qualification points. He tied two Birmingham defenders in knots before letting rip with another long-range beauty that won the match and lit up the Lane. His repertoire of goals was growing ever more impressive, and he was drawing praise from all quarters. Not only was Santini delighted with his young striker, but Birmingham manager Steve Bruce held his hands up after the game and admitted that he was just too good for them on the day.

It was not quite enough to gain Defoe a starting place in England's first qualifier, against Austria in Vienna. Instead, Sven-Göran Eriksson chose Alan Smith to play alongside Michael Owen at the top of the England team. It was to be a night of disappointment for England as they surrendered a two-goal lead to draw 2-2. It was the sort of capitulation that

Defoe had seen two seasons earlier as West Ham had crumbled to Premier League relegation. It was not helped by a disastrous display in goal by David James, another involved in that dark season at Upton Park.

A third former Hammer, Joe Cole, was sent on alongside Defoe late in the game as Eriksson took a gamble to claw back the victory that England looked so certain to claim. It nearly paid off when Defoe went clean through on goal, only to be denied by the upright with the goalkeeper beaten. It ended up being a frustrating draw for an England team that should have won the game with little trouble. Any international manager will say there are no easy games at that level, but Eriksson knew his team should have been heading to Poland with three points under their belt instead of one.

The Swede took measures to ensure the same problem would not befall his team again. He made the changes that both pundits and fans wanted to see. The struggling James was replaced by Tottenham's Paul Robinson, and another Spurs player by the name of Jermain Defoe came into the side for his full England debut. Having seen him play and score on several occasions, Sven had finally given Defoe the opportunity he deserved.

Poland were simply not used to someone like Defoe. Their defenders had never come up against a player who could cause them so many problems. His pace was frightening, his trickery unpredictable and his shooting unstoppable. All three attributes were proven in one moment ten minutes before half-time. Speeding into the penalty area to receive the ball after good work from David Beckham and John Terry, he turned his marker in the blink of an eye and rifled a missile of a shot beyond goalkeeper Jerzy Dudek. It was Defoe's first England goal and it had come on his full international debut. He had done it again.

It was an emotional moment for him. His mother had been with him every step of the way and she had flown to Poland to see him in action. How thrilled she must have been to see her boy do her proud again. Defoe recalled in an interview with the *Independent*: 'When I scored I really could have just dropped to the ground and cried. I've pictured that so many times in my head. When I first got the call-up I was just picturing myself scoring for England. The same just before the game. So when it happened, it really was just unbelievable.'

England won the game 2-1, and the goal would mean so much to Defoe. It was as though it vindicated the decisions that many had questioned. Was it right to choose West Ham over Charlton? Was it right to leave West Ham in the way that he did? Was it right to put his own career first? When that shot hit the back of the net in Chorzow it was as though every choice was proven right. His aim had been to become an England international and he had now fulfilled that aim. But Defoe knew that there was more to come, and so did Eriksson, who described Defoe as 'a great talent' and suggested he would always score goals. It would cement his place in the national squad – for the time being at least.

When Defoe returned to domestic matters with Spurs, he found that scoring goals would not get any easier, despite the England coach's words. Two consecutive goalless draws would highlight Tottenham's inconsistency once again, although they maintained their unbeaten start to the league season. Indeed it was in a League Cup tie that he and the team would remember how to score. The north Londoners travelled to Oldham and went goal crazy, Defoe sweeping home the last in a 6-0 hammering. The result must have been doubly sweet after the previous time he had faced Oldham, when they had embarrassed West Ham in the same competition two years earlier.

Defoe would return to England duty in mid-October with two more appearances in qualifier matches, firstly against Wales at Old Trafford and then against Azerbaijan in Baku. He would play both games from the start, but would not have the same impact as he had in his last outing. This was thanks in part to the coach's attempt to incorporate Defoe, Owen and Rooney into England's starting line-up. While this might have seemed like a positive move for Defoe in that it created another place for a forward, it only served to complicate matters as it forced him to occupy a wider position in which he would not operate so effectively. It showed in both games, as Defoe was eventually replaced after struggling to come to terms with the new system.

Those struggles would continue as two defeats in a row for Tottenham tempered their impressive start to the season. However, again the League Cup would provide an upturn in fortunes with a trip to Bolton, who had just beaten them at White Hart Lane. Having scored his most recent Tottenham goal in the previous round, Defoe now netted an equaliser with another long-distance strike of genuine class. Spurs needed another leveller late in the day to take the match into extra time, when two more goals saw them through, the second of which came from Defoe as he finished off Robbie Keane's pass from ten yards. Although Les Ferdinand rolled back the years with a third Bolton goal, it was Tottenham's night as they returned to winning ways and Defoe got back among the goals.

But again inconsistency would prove to be the team's weakness, and things were not helped when Santini walked out of the club following a defeat at Fulham. This represented a potential blow for Defoe after all the good words Santini had been moved to say about his number one goal threat. Martin Jol was put in temporary charge as Spurs looked to get their season back on track in another London derby against Defoe's old masters, Charlton.

Regardless of circumstances, this was a home game that Spurs were expected to win. But things did not go according to plan and by half-time they were 2-0 down and booed off the pitch by their furious supporters. Once more defensive frailties were being exposed and the team were lacking any real direction. Without a manager as the halfway point in the season approached, they were in need of inspiration, but all they got in the second half was more irritation. A third Charlton goal effectively put the game beyond the home side, and while Robbie Keane's penalty narrowed the deficit before a blistering Defoe shot on the turn gave the scoreline an element of respectability, it was clear Tottenham were in trouble.

Knowing that major upheaval would not be the answer midway through a season that was already looking shaky, the Tottenham board acted quickly to give Jol the manager's job on a full-time basis. It was a decision that proved popular with the fans and appeared to have the support of the players as they prepared for the next round of the League Cup at Burnley. For Defoe, it would be a familiar situation – the Dutchman was the tenth manager he had played under in his professional career.

But Defoe was happy to show yet another manager why he

was developing a reputation, with one of his trademark 25-yard thunderbolts. It was the third and final goal of a comfortable Spurs win, following two goals from his strike partner Robbie Keane, and sent the Tottenham fans home with smiles on their faces. It was the kind of tonic that was needed after two straight defeats had dropped them to mid-table, and they would need to be in a positive frame of mind. Their next game would be against Arsenal, back at White Hart Lane.

North London derbies are never small games. This most intense of rivalries normally has enough ingredients to be one of the tastiest encounters of any season. However, Arsenal had won the Premier League the previous season without losing, and had only just had their (still unsurpassed) record of 49 league games without defeat ended. Both sides were desperate for the points, so this particular north London derby looked like being one of the biggest yet. Not only was it one of the biggest, it proved to be one of the best.

As a boyhood Gooner, Defoe was only too aware of the intense rivalry between the two clubs. Now, for the first time, he would be at the very centre of it all – although perhaps not on the side of the divide he might have wanted some years ago. Nevertheless he was now a Tottenham player and determined to put the team he had supported as a child to the sword.

He did not disappoint. Even though Arsenal eventually won the game by an astonishing 5-4 scoreline, Defoe shared the scoresheet with such Premier League legends as Thierry Henry, Patrick Vieira, Freddie Ljungberg and Robert Pires. Not only did he share a platform with them, he outshone them all with the goal of the game. Picking the ball up inside the

Arsenal half, he set off on a run that took him away from four Gunners defenders before driving an unstoppable shot into the top corner from just inside the penalty area. It was pure inspiration from the England man. Tottenham's new manager might be fuming with his defenders, but he described his strikers as 'terrific' after the game – a clear indication that he felt Defoe was up there with the best in the league.

And so it proved, as Defoe was again included in the national party to play a friendly international in Spain. However, what should have been a marvellous occasion would prove to be one of the worst nights in the striker's career – and not for any footballing reason.

Spain's coach Luis Aragones had made headlines in the build-up to the game with comments of flagrant ignorance, describing Arsenal and France striker Thierry Henry as 'that black shit'. His comments would have an appalling influence on what was to come at Real Madrid's Bernabeu stadium. England lost the game 1-0 but that was of little significance.

Early in the game, a strong challenge by Arsenal defender Ashley Cole was met with a chorus of monkey noises and chants from the home crowd. It was one of the worst displays of racism in an international fixture seen in years. Cole was not the only recipient. For the remainder of the game he, Shaun Wright-Phillips and substitutes Defoe and Jermaine Jenas were targeted by this vile abuse.

It was something that stayed with Defoe for some time. 'The game against Spain was horrible,' he recalled some months later. 'I'm only young and so are Ashley Cole, Shaun Wright-Phillips and Jermaine Jenas. You want to play football at special places like the Bernabeu and you want to remember it. But when I think about it now, what can I say? I can turn round and say to people, "I have played at the Bernabeu". But it wasn't a special night because of what happened, with the abuse and all that. It was tarnished.'

Thankfully, it was an episode that Defoe could put behind him quickly as Tottenham got back to Premier League business. A disappointing defeat at Aston Villa had made it five straight losses in the league, but Defoe was on hand to help put that stretch to bed with the next game at home to Middlesbrough, although he would also earn the wrath of his manager.

Defoe opened the scoring in Tottenham's 2-0 win at White Hart Lane, but was booked for his goal celebration when he removed his shirt to reveal a vest emblazoned with the message 'Happy Birthday Baby' for his watching girlfriend. The yellow card was his fifth of the season and brought him a suspension. Martin Jol was furious, especially as Defoe had been cautioned for taking off his shirt on the opening day of the season. 'It is amazing,' Jol told reporters after the game. 'They get told about it and we have talked about it and then he comes out and does it again. He thinks it is the right manner to celebrate but we will miss him next week. We have to talk to him again. He can't do that. He plays for our team and he is important. Having a message under his shirt is even worse.'

Part of his anger was because Jol was fully aware of how good a striker Defoe was becoming. 'You know how he takes his goals,' he added. 'He is decisive. He shoots and he scores goals, though as I have said before, he can still improve.'

Jol had laid down the challenge, and it was up to Defoe to take it up. He would do that in the quarter-finals of the League Cup with another goal, but this time it was another

Spurs striker's turn to lose his head and cause frustration. Defoe came on as a second-half substitute and looked to have done enough to send Tottenham through as he finished from Freddie Kanoute's cross in the second half of extra time. However, Kanoute would spoil his hard work as he inexplicably handled a Liverpool corner to give away a penalty with just two minutes to go. It was converted to send the tie to spot-kicks. It was a fate Defoe was used to in this competition, and again he would be on the receiving end of defeat as Liverpool shattered any dreams of a trip to the Millennium Stadium. His former Hammers companion Kanoute was one of two Spurs players to miss in the shoot-out.

A disappointing night at the Lane, then, but only a minor blip as Tottenham finished 2004 in style with three wins and a draw in their final four games of the calendar year. After beating Blackburn at Ewood Park, Defoe would be back at the top of his game with a hat-trick in a 5-1 thrashing of Southampton at the Lane. His first goal was a smart finish after good work from Kanoute. His second was a piece of ruthless opportunism, capitalising on a hospital pass by Paul Telfer to fire home. His third was a true poacher's goal as he pounced on a rebound to find the net again. With January looming there would be more speculation about his future. The big clubs were rumoured to be circling again.

'We are certain we can keep hold of him,' said Jol. 'He has a long contract and he is happy with the club. We can go places with him.' High praise indeed, and the feeling was mutual as Defoe paid a heartfelt tribute to the Dutchman who was really starting to get the best out of his striker. Defoe added: 'The manager is such a strong character and he expects

110 per cent. He's a nice man, he encourages you, and you can relate to him. He's a very good coach with good ideas, and he gets you going before matches. You can see a massive difference since he's come in. Even in training he expects players to do well and he pushes you hard. I'm young, I've still got a lot to learn and he's what I needed.'

There was little doubt, then, that Defoe would remain a Tottenham player for the foreseeable future. He was happy, he was scoring goals and, crucially, the manager was delighted with him. His confidence would show in the last game of 2004 with a 20-yard opener in a 1-1 draw with Crystal Palace. It was not the ideal result in a game that Spurs should have won, but it was another game unbeaten, making it six without loss. That ensured they would finish 2004 in eighth place – very much on course for their dream of European football.

2005 would begin slowly for Defoe. Despite Spurs' unbeaten run continuing for two more games before ending at home to Chelsea, he would not score again until the end of January in a controversial 1-1 draw at West Brom in the fourth round of the FA Cup. And the controversy was down to him.

It was not the first time Defoe had been accused of going down easily when a challenge from Baggies defender Darren Purse sent him tumbling in the box. Despite the home side's protests, the referee pointed to the spot and the striker dusted himself down to smash the ball into the net. The West Brom players and management were furious. Purse was convinced that he had not touched Defoe and made his feelings known after the game. Martin Jol did what any manager would do and defended his player, saying he was not a cheat. Was it really a dive? Only one person knew for sure. But a penalty was given and his strike was his 16th of the season – his best haul so far.

He would make it 17 at Bolton back in the Premier League with a nice goal. Having come on as a substitute with 25 minutes left, he took the ball round defender Tal Ben Haim and just beat keeper Jussi Jaaskelainen. However, Spurs were already three goals down by then and as a result slipped to ninth in the table. However, the following comfortable 3-1 win at home to Portsmouth, where Defoe would notch an assist, was a clear sign that his game had continued to develop. Not only was he scoring goals, he was bringing his team-mates into play and making goals for them as well.

It was his continued good form that was keeping him in Sven-Göran Eriksson's thoughts for the England squad. However, there would be no match time for Defoe in the next game – a friendly against Holland at Villa Park. Instead he remained on the bench with the coach choosing to bring on Crystal Palace striker Andy Johnson for his international debut on the right of an experimental 4-3-3 attacking line. Defoe might not have appeared in the goalless draw, but it would be a poignant occasion for him, and the other players abused in England's match against Spain, as both teams wore shirts bearing anti-racism messages.

No appearance and therefore no goal, but that would not stop Defoe's international stock from rising. His next game was Tottenham's FA Cup replay against West Brom back at the Lane. While the first game had brought the striker some headlines he had not wanted, there was no question after this game that he would be one of the most talked-about England players for the right reasons. And again, he did it in front of the England coach, whose visits to north London were becoming more and more regular.

Former Arsenal striker Nwankwo Kanu gave the Albion a shock lead, but all that seemed to do was spark the hosts into life. After Robbie Keane had levelled with a penalty in the dying seconds of the first half, Defoe took it upon himself to see off the West Midlanders almost single-handedly. His first goal was drilled home from the edge of the box five minutes after the interval, and five minutes later he was on the end of some good work from Kanoute to round off the scoring. He was simply unplayable, drawing praise from Tottenham's sporting director Frank Arnesen.

Arnesen had joined Spurs in the summer as part of the new-look management team. He had worked as technical director at PSV Eindhoven, and in that capacity had discovered such modern greats as Romario, Ronaldo and Ruud van Nistelrooy. It is fair to say the Dane knows a thing or two about strikers, so it was no small matter when he said after the game: 'Defoe is Defoe and there isn't a second Defoe. When he gets a chance, bang. He always hits the target.

'He doesn't need time or space to hit the ball, and has power in both feet,' he added. 'Give him the ball in and around the box and he's unbelievable. Defoe is up there with the best strikers I've seen – and he's still only 22.' If Defoe was unsure of how far he had come in such a short space of time, these words from his club's most knowledgeable student of the European game must have convinced him he was going very much in the right direction.

In addition he had now scored ten FA Cup goals in just nine ties since starting his career. That would become 11 in his next outing as Spurs travelled to Nottingham Forest. Not only was it another goal, but it was another kind of goal for the young striker. This time, with 45 minutes on the clock, he scored direct from a free-kick. However, Defoe could not take all the credit as his shot didn't seem to carry any real threat until rookie keeper Colin Doyle let the ball squirm through his fingers and into the net. This moment of good fortune for Defoe extended his rich vein of goalscoring to five in his last five Tottenham games. It was also another milestone: for the first time in his professional career he had reached 20 goals in a season.

What goes up, however, must come down. Defoe now went on a four-game run without scoring (five if you include an unused substitute's appearance) as Spurs lost two Premier League games in a row and crashed out of the FA Cup by a single goal at Newcastle. With no chance of any silverware and now down to tenth place in the league, the club's only focus now was to force their way up the league and get into Europe by finishing in the top six. It was not going to be an easy task and Defoe knew the only way to help his team progress was to get back on the goal trail.

Manchester City were the visitors to White Hart Lane as Defoe did just that, albeit in somewhat bizarre fashion. He was involved in the build-up when he inadvertently miscued his attempt to score from Andy Reid's low cross from the left. The ball eventually broke to Simon Davies but his wild shot carried no danger until it hit Defoe, who had managed to turn his head towards goal and just control his movement enough to divert the ball over the line. It was certainly not a goal resulting from hours of work on the training ground, but they all count. City did equalise but Robbie Keane was on hand to snatch the points for Spurs as they reached seventh with eight games remaining.

The end of March again Defoe saw on international duty with England in another pair of World Cup qualifying matches, the first at Old Trafford against Northern Ireland followed by a trip to St James' Park to take on Azerbaijan. England were expected to win both games with little trouble and they did so, with Defoe featuring briefly in both games. He only played ten minutes of the 4-0 mauling of Northern Ireland, but received a little more playing time against Azerbaijan, when he managed to show some nice touches in his cameo appearance in the 2-0 victory.

While Defoe had not scored for England since his first international goal in Poland at the start of the season, it was clear that Eriksson thought enough of him to continue using him in important games. With more caps came more experience of international level, which would stand him in good stead for the remaining qualifiers when injuries and suspensions would start to take their toll.

But Defoe's lack of goals in international football was mirrored by goals in domestic football drying up as well. He would only score one more all season, in an April clash with Newcastle at White Hart Lane, and like his goal against Manchester City, it was somewhat fortuitous. After a simple backpass from Celestine Babayaro, Magpies keeper Steve Harper scuffed his clearance straight to Simon Davies, who flicked the ball back towards goal. Defoe was waiting, having been kept onside by Babayaro, and was able to roll the ball into the net before Harper could get back into position. It was a crucial win for Spurs as they clung to seventh spot.

Unfortunately, Tottenham would only win one more game that season, as three draws and two defeats saw them slip to ninth place in the Premier League, where they would finish.

There was to be no dream ticket to Europe. That said, there had been progress since the season started back in August. From mid-table obscurity one year to European contention the next showed that Tottenham were making strides.

For Defoe the season would end with a further piece of positive news. Despite newspaper reports linking him with a summer move to Chelsea, he made the choice that fans in the Lilywhite half of north London wanted to hear. He signed a new four-and-a-half year contract and pledged his immediate future to the club, to the clear delight of Martin Jol. The Tottenham boss had challenged Defoe to get even better, and it must have been a joy to the manager to see his striker take that challenge on. Defoe said on the day: 'It is a very special day for me, and this season has been special as well. I think we've got a strong squad, pushed on and done really well. Everything about the club is great at the moment.'

It had been a fantastic season for Defoe. In his first full season in a Spurs shirt he had managed to score 22 goals and make himself a regular in the England squad. He had also netted his first international goal and had become the subject of increased attention from the England coaching staff, who appeared to be viewing him as a serious long-term player for the national team.

This was exemplified by Defoe being picked for the England squad for a brief summer tour of the United States that would include games against the USA and Colombia. Again, Defoe would be restricted to two substitute appearances but his continued presence in the squad was evidence of his place in Sven-Göran Eriksson's thoughts. The following season would be massive for the national team. If the qualifiers continued to go to plan, there would be the reward of the World Cup finals in Germany. This meant that each individual would need to prove their worth for both club and country throughout the entire season, and each individual would be desperate to do so. Jermain Defoe would be no different.

Chapter 6

Germany
Or Bust

If there's one sure-fire way for a striker to get himself noticed by the national team's management during a World Cup selection season, it's to score a goal on the opening day. Better yet, score a goal with someone from the national team's management there to see it. Especially if Sven-Göran Eriksson has been to watch your club play a pre-season friendly against FC Porto but left before his potential star has scored two impressive goals.

However, with his assistant Tord Grip looking on during Spurs' visit to Portsmouth on a rain-soaked summer's day, Eriksson was about to get another glowing report of a young man, edging towards 23 years of age, whose knocking on the England door was turning into a steady hammering.

Defoe scored one and made another as Tottenham cruised to a 2-0 win at Fratton Park. First he was on hand to provide a delicious cross into the area which Pompey defender Andy

Griffin could only turn into his own net as Egyptian striker Mido threatened. Then he appeared in the Portsmouth area seemingly out of nowhere to nip the ball around goalkeeper Sander Westerveld and seal all three points. It was a real opportunist's goal, and one of such quality that Spurs manager Martin Jol was left purring. 'I looked up and saw two Portsmouth defenders and I thought Jermain wasn't even looking at the goal,' he said. 'But he was on to the chance – and that is the difference between himself and other strikers.' Once again Defoe's eye for goal was being singled out.

Defoe's performance could have been even better had he taken the other chances that came his way, but with match sharpness understandably lacking on the first game after the summer break, he had done himself no harm at all. He had scored 14 goals in the Premier League the previous season, which led him to set himself the target of going one better for the season ahead. Such a haul would surely be enough to gain him a seat on the plane for Germany and the biggest football extravaganza of them all.

In the more immediate future, Defoe's exploits would earn him a seat on the plane for England's friendly in Denmark. He would also be awarded a start ahead of Three Lions regular Michael Owen, who was struggling to settle at Real Madrid. Defoe's partner would be Wayne Rooney – the man whom Eriksson had seen score for Manchester United while his right hand man was at Portsmouth – but it was to be another frustrating affair in the national colours for the Spurs man.

Defoe managed the best chance of the first half with a poorly struck volley that was comfortably saved by the Danish keeper. However, his overall performance had not been anywhere near inadequate and it was a surprise when he was sacrificed at half-time to make way for Owen. That decision looked even more bizarre as a dismal second-half collapse ended in a shock 4-1 defeat for the visitors.

It was a disappointing moment for Defoe, who was being noticed not only for his goals, but the way he was scoring them. Players like Rooney had the technical ability and the likes of Heskey had the strength, but since Owen had moved to Spain there were very few players on home soil who had such a level of single-mindedness in front of goal. Defoe deserved the opportunity to show what he could do at the highest level, but again that opportunity had been only be a fleeting one. Luckily, it was only the first week of the football season. It was time to focus on club matters.

Tottenham's ninth-place finish in the previous campaign had received mixed reviews. It was certainly a marked improvement on the season before, but the fact remained that at one point Spurs had pole position for sixth and a place in the UEFA Cup. That they had failed to achieve this was seen as a failure by many of the White Hart Lane faithful. However, it seemed that in Martin Jol, both players and fans had a manager they could unite behind.

His first full season in charge brought some changes to the squad, with Frederic Kanoute eventually departing to Sevilla. But Jol bolstered the group with big-money signing Jermaine Jenas from Newcastle, and a world-famous name in Edgar Davids from Inter Milan, to add bite in midfield. Not only were fans and players united, they were excited as well. 'I don't want to say too much about our chances this season,' said Defoe after the Portsmouth game. 'But I think we've got the strength in depth now to do well.'

One thing was certain: if Tottenham were going to make a genuine push for European football, they would need Defoe firing on all cylinders. The first home game of the season, against Middlesbrough, was the perfect opportunity to carry on the good work he had started at Portsmouth before the international break. And guess who was in the crowd to watch?

After giving Defoe only half the game in Copenhagen, Eriksson saw just how lethal a weapon he could be when unleashed for longer. Standing just five feet and seven inches tall, one of the smallest players on the pitch displayed awesome feats of pace and power that rocked Middlesbrough to the core. Five minutes into the second half he picked up the ball just inside his own half before setting off on a rampaging run through the heart of his opposition. He tore into the visiting side's half, evaded a challenge from Gareth Southgate and let fly from 25 yards. The net nearly came out of the ground.

That remarkable strike was followed up by another assist for Mido to wrap up the points. It capped a special performance from Defoe, who had put his England disappointment behind him to give Sven more food for thought. Steve McLaren, then Boro boss, was on the England coaching staff and admitted Defoe's supreme performance came from something deep within. Perhaps it came from a level of determination and steel that came from wanting to prove he was good enough for 90 minutes with England every time.

But first he had to ensure he was getting 90 minutes every time with Spurs. After two games Defoe had fired the Lilywhites to the top of the Premier League but it was still not enough for Martin Jol, who made the controversial decision to replace the man in form with Robbie Keane for the visit to

Blackburn – a call he made just an hour before kick-off. It was a decision made to look all the more strange when Defoe was given only ten minutes to make an impact in a dull, goalless game. Suffice it to say the impact never came.

Perhaps Jol was keeping Defoe fresh for Tottenham's next game in the Premier League, at home to London rivals Chelsea. The striker came back into the starting line-up and displayed his usual sharpness against Jose Mourinho's big-money superstars. He very nearly gave his side the lead, stinging the palms of Blues goalkeeper Petr Cech with a volleyed snapshot. But in the end he failed to score as Spurs suffered their first defeat of the season. It was to prove a costly blank with two World Cup qualifiers on the way and Michael Owen suspended.

Instead of bringing in Defoe as a straight replacement for Owen, Sven opted to take on Wales in Cardiff with the 4-3-3 formation he had been testing in recent international fixtures. However, instead of playing as one of the three strikers, Defoe had to make do with a place on the bench. This time he was given 20 minutes to shine as a replacement for Shaun Wright-Phillips but he had little opportunity to make his presence felt in a very tight game that England were grateful to win, thanks to a solitary Joe Cole strike.

Owen was restored to the side for the trip to Northern Ireland, meaning that Defoe would again have to be content with a place in reserve. He was brought on late in the game under abysmal circumstances and again was given no real opportunity to show the coach what he could do. However, Eriksson had bigger worries. England, against all the odds and to their huge embarrassment, lost the game by a goal to nil. It was one of the worst nights in the national team's recent history, and Defoe was a part of it. That night at Windsor Park will never be forgotten.

While the plight of England was scrutinised down to the tiniest detail by the British media and the national coach was dealt the traditional helping of hyperbolic criticism, Defoe set about his task of playing for Tottenham with his usual gusto. While he did not score in Spurs' home fixture against Liverpool, he was a constant threat for the entire game. His running caused no end of problems for the Reds' back line and he went close on a number of occasions. He was certainly the outstanding Tottenham performer on the day as his latest strike partner, Grzegorz Rasiak, a new signing from Derby County and a Polish international, failed to make a significant impression on the game.

However, the manager would stick with the pairing. He had already decided that in Robbie Keane and Jermain Defoe he had two excellent strikers, but two small strikers. They were too similar in the Dutchman's eyes and he felt a physical presence was needed alongside one of them in order to thrive. It was a continuation of the idea that Glenn Roeder had championed while Defoe was a West Ham player.

In fact, the first time Defoe and Keane did play alongside each other, the end result seemed to prove Jol's point in emphatic manner. A trip to the seaside ended in despair as Spurs crashed out of the League Cup at the home of League Two side Grimsby Town. Defoe missed more than his fair share of chances but it was Keane who suffered the disappointment of being dropped for the following league game, another London derby at home to Fulham.

This time Defoe's foil would be the enigmatic Mido in another little-and-large combination following the Egyptian's return from suspension. Defoe would repay his manager's faith in style as he lashed home the winning goal with a first-time left-footed strike that left Fulham goalkeeper Tony Warner with no chance. Warner would fare better soon after as the Spurs forward pair combined brilliantly, Defoe's rapid turn and pass finding Mido whose shot was well saved. It was more than enough to show the manager the two should keep their places for the next derby, at Defoe's first stomping ground.

Charlton will never again be a place where Jermain Defoe is made to feel welcome. As irritated as their fans will forever be at his decision to leave the club as a teenager, their mood will never be helped by the fear that more often than not he will do something on the pitch to rub salt in the wound. This October encounter was no different as Defoe had a hand in the winning goal, scored by his striking rival Keane. After coming from two goals down to level, Spurs were in the ascendancy when substitute Keane picked out Defoe inside the box. Instead of going for goal himself, he showed remarkable composure to slide the ball back to the Irishman who hammered in the winner. Who said the two little men could not play in the same team?

Well, Martin Jol did. It would remain the case that Defoe would be Jol's preferred option as the little man in his team. However, it would also remain the case that the little man would not get much of a chance for England, particularly as Michael Owen was still very much the first choice in that particular role. This time Liverpool striker Peter Crouch would be his partner and, at six feet seven inches, it looked like the little and large double act was in Sven-Göran Eriksson's thoughts too, although he was not ready to reunite the former England Under-21 strike partnership just yet.

Crouch was instrumental in winning the penalty that sealed England's 1-0 win against Austria before Rooney returned to partner Owen in a 2-1 victory at home to Poland. Defoe remained on the substitutes' bench for the entire duration of both games but, much to everyone in the country's relief, the six points fired England through to the World Cup finals as group winners. While Defoe had not been able to play as much as a part as he would have liked, at least he had something else to play for when he returned to club action.

As expected, he began that process with a starting place for Spurs as they entertained Everton. The task for Tottenham was becoming clear – exploit the poor start to the season from bitter rivals Arsenal and steal their place in the Champions League by finishing the season in fourth place. With an impressive set of results under their belts already and only one league defeat (by reigning champions Chelsea), they had certainly put themselves in a great position to do so. If the performances continued at this level, it would be difficult for anybody to stop them, as Everton found out at White Hart Lane in October.

Defoe and Mido were Jol's chosen pairing and the two of them set about earning three more points with great aplomb. It was Mido who gave Spurs the lead, but only after Defoe had alerted Everton to what they could expect with a spectacular piece of trickery that left Toffees defender Matteo Ferrari tackling into thin air before unleashing an awesome strike that former England keeper Nigel Martyn needed all his years of experience to keep out. Defoe was at the heart of things again as he made the goal that cemented all three points. After collecting the ball on the left he set off on another mesmerising run and his cross for Jermaine Jenas was perfect, allowing the former Newcastle midfielder to score his first goal for Tottenham and send them up to second in the table.

It was a good place to be, as their next outing was to the home of Manchester United. Tottenham had never won at Old Trafford in the Premier League but it was also a place where Defoe was no stranger to finding the net. Typically, neither Spurs nor Defoe would succeed – but both club and player left the North West relatively happy with how the day had gone for them.

United took an expected early lead through an unexpected goalscorer in French defender Mikael Silvestre, but it was far from an easy ride for the Premier League's most imposing juggernaut. Perhaps that is what they should have expected – after all, Tottenham were sitting proudly above them in the league standings. Defoe could well have grabbed the equaliser himself just moments before half-time when his rasping 25-yard drive took an awkward bounce in front of keeper Edwin Van der Sar, but the Dutchman did enough to keep the ball out. But he could do nothing about the second-half leveller. Defoe managed to draw a foul from his former West Ham team-mate Rio Ferdinand on the very edge of the penalty area, and Jenas stunned Old Trafford with a beautifully curled equaliser. Jenas had scored twice in two games, and both goals had been created by Defoe. He was proving to anyone watching on that his contribution to a team was about more than just scoring.

The draw at Manchester United was followed by another 1-1 draw with rivals Arsenal at the Lane. Again Defoe would impress with a tireless performance that brought the best out of the Gunners defenders. Again, however, there would be no goal for Defoe. The points dropped saw Tottenham slip to third, but it still kept them well above Arsenal heading into November. Not only that, they had now played each of the Premier League's 'big four' and only lost one game, against Chelsea. Spurs had never looked in better shape to break the Champions League hold that the Blues, Manchester United, Liverpool and Arsenal had.

They were also seven games without defeat in the League, although that run would end in controversial circumstances at Bolton – and Defoe would be right in the middle of that controversy. Minutes after the hosts had taken the lead through Kevin Nolan, Defoe had a perfectly good goal disallowed for offside, with television replays proving that he was onside by a considerable margin. Both he and Martin Jol were rightly furious, and even Trotters manager Sam Allardyce accepted that his team had got lucky. It was not the time to see a legitimate goal chalked off with Mr Eriksson watching from the stands ahead of England's friendly with Argentina in Geneva.

The international was to be another game in which Eriksson would name Defoe on the bench and it was another game in which Eriksson would not use him. With Rooney and Owen both fit and firing, they proved that they were the men to be dislodged. Owen scored twice while Rooney was a constant threat in an impressive 3-2 win over the South Americans.

Things did not get easier for Defoe. Next he was unexpectedly left on the bench for Tottenham's home game, against West Ham. His misery was compounded by the Hammers fans who unleashed a barrage of abuse at him. Still bitter about his departure, they taunted him with their chants of 'Judas', 'scum' and 'you're just a small Paul Ince' (a reference to Ince's controversial departure from Upton Park after being pictured in a Manchester United shirt – before he had signed for them).

Defoe did get on in the latter stages but was denied a chance to win the game when Mido went for goal himself instead of opting for an easier pass. It was another 1-1 draw for Tottenham when it could have been more, and it was another major frustration for Defoe, who found himself on the bench again for the trip to Wigan. Spurs won the game 2-1 and Jol commented after the game that there was little between Defoe and Keane (who had started in his place), and rotating the two strikers would benefit the Englishman in the future. While it was a bad day for Defoe, there was no doubt that Keane had performed well in his place.

As a result Keane kept his place and he scored again as Tottenham got back into the top four with a 3-2 win at home to Sunderland. He could have had a second had he scored a late penalty, an incident which delayed Defoe's entry to the game – he was just about to replace the Irishman. The England striker responded in the only way he knew how in the game that followed, a home encounter against Portsmouth. The visitors had taken the lead in the first half but Ledley King's equaliser and Mido's late penalty put Tottenham ahead before substitute Defoe reminded everyone what he had become famous for. A display of pace left Pompey defender Andy Griffin trailing in his wake before he fired home a low finish to seal the points.

It was still not enough to earn a start. Keane and Mido would be among the scorers again as Tottenham drew 3-3 at Middlesbrough. Having come on as a second-half substitute, Defoe left the field in the last minute with a nasty-looking ankle injury, prompting fears he would be out for two weeks.

Fortunately he was back within the week, coming off the bench again on Boxing Day against Birmingham City to score his fifth of the season in injury time. It was a goal of true style, Defoe finding space in the area and beating his man with some neat stopovers before lashing the ball into the roof of the net. It sealed a 2-0 win for Spurs but it was to be Defoe's last goal of the calendar year.

It was a shame, as Defoe's impressive cameos from the bench had convinced Martin Jol that he was deserving of a place in the starting line-up as Tottenham were starting to make genuine headway in their quest for Champions League football. Jol had spoken earlier in the season about the team making strides towards Europe but had so far stayed quiet over whether or not they could reach the premier club competition. However, having spent the last four games in fourth position, even the Dutchman must have been starting to think that it might just be Tottenham's year.

If he really was thinking that, he would come back down to earth with a bump in the next game, against West Brom on his old stomping ground at the Hawthorns. Defoe was back in the team but could do nothing to prevent Spurs falling to a disappointing 2-0 reverse. It might have been different had his penalty appeal after being felled by Neil Clement not been dismissed by referee Mike Riley. Grzegorz Rasiak was given his first start in over three months alongside Defoe but the partnership never seemed to click on a disappointing day for the north London club.

The disappointment would continue for Defoe as he was once again on the bench for Newcastle's visit to White Hart Lane. Goals from Teemu Tainio and Mido grabbed the points but Defoe had little chance to make his presence felt when he eventually replaced Keane with only ten minutes left. However, there was plenty to be positive about as 2005 drew to a close. Tottenham were still in fourth and looking a good bet for Champions League football next season, while England had qualified for the World Cup finals in Germany. While things may not have been ideal for Defoe, he knew there would be plenty to play for in 2006. A regular in the England squad, if not always playing, and knowing that his club manager saw him very much as a part of his plans, the young and talented striker had it all to play for. But to have it all to play for, you have to get the chance play.

Chances, unfortunately, were few and far between. Defoe's start in the defeat at West Brom was only his first in seven games and again he faced an extended run on the bench. Despite coming into the season on fine form, the goals seemed to have dried up for him, and with Tottenham in their strongest league position for a number of years, the manager had a decision to make. He knew Defoe was a precocious talent with plenty of goals under his belt already and plenty more still to come, but the recent exploits of Mido and Keane were impossible to ignore. Jol knew he could not keep everyone happy, but if the team kept winning his hands would be tied. He had already decided that it would be either Keane or Defoe, not both, so it was quite simply a case of whoever was scoring goals was going to play. Recent form suggested that it quite simply had to be Keane.

So as 2006 began Defoe was still amongst the substitutes in Tottenham's first match of the year against Manchester City at Eastlands. Spurs would get themselves another victory to remain in that fourth spot and, tellingly, the goals were scored by Mido and Keane. But Jol remained coy on his team's chances of reaching the Champions League. 'You never know,' he told the media after the game. 'We have 40 points and have scored over 30 goals, which is pretty good.' Of those goals, however, only five had come from the boot of Defoe, whose chances to impress the England coaching staff were beginning to run out.

His luck would not change in the FA Cup, as he was left out again as Spurs crashed to a demoralising 3-2 defeat at Leicester after leading by two goals. With the score level at 20 minutes to go, Defoe came on and almost got his team a place in the fourth round with an inventive chip towards goal that dropped just over the crossbar. It was the closest they had come to scoring before Mark de Vries slotted in an injury-time winner to end Tottenham's cup interests for another year. That left only the league, which was fine for the team in terms of their priorities, but it was a nightmare for Defoe. It meant he would have even fewer chances to impress.

The Leicester defeat had clearly affected the team, as they went to Anfield and struggled to find any rhythm against a Liverpool side who had top four aspirations of their own. Defoe would again be restricted to an appearance in the final quarter of the game but he was dealt with effectively by the defensive pairing of Sami Hyypia and Jamie Carragher. A single goal was enough to condemn the visitors to their fourth defeat of the season.

After two defeats in a row, Jol decided it was time for a change against Aston Villa. Oddly, he went against his own philosophy and played Keane and Defoe together from the start. While this was a popular choice with the fans, they would leave White Hart Lane feeling frustrated once again as the duo failed to gel in a 0-0 draw that should really have ended with Spurs taking all three points. Both men were guilty of missing chances, although this was down in part to some fabulous goalkeeping from Thomas Sorensen, as Tottenham failed to capitalise on Arsenal's defeat to Everton earlier in the day.

Jol was beginning to worry about the lack of goals. 'We did everything right, did everything we could have done except score,' he said. 'It was a great opportunity to open up a gap on Arsenal and we have blown it.' Strong words from the manager, who had hauled Defoe off for the final stages of the game after another quiet display. It would see him relegated to the bench yet again.

Spurs lost the next game against Fulham 1-0 at Craven Cottage to extend their worrying run to two defeats in three games. However, if there was any positive to take for Defoe, it was that his performance off the bench for the last 20 minutes was enough to convince the manager that he should be back in the starting line-up. Tottenham had offered very little going forward, but Defoe's presence had almost gained them an unlikely win.

He produced their first shot on target of the game as late as the 81st minute when he forced keeper Antti Niemi into a smart save, and could have had a penalty after racing into the area and going down under a challenge from Carlos Bocanegra. Referee Howard Webb rejected Tottenham's appeals and Bocanegra compounded their misery with the winning goal in the dying seconds.

While it was another disappointing result for Spurs, it had been an encouraging performance from Defoe. Without a goal in his last seven appearances for the club, there was little doubt that his confidence would be affected. However, he had displayed enough in his most recent showing from the bench to be restored to the starting eleven. It was a just reward for the striker, who had done little to deserve losing his spot in the first place. Jol had had no choice but to play Keane and Mido while they were scoring goals, but once that changed he had the perfect replacement waiting in the wings. Defoe was back where he wanted to be, and at the perfect time too – Tottenham's next game was at home to Charlton.

As if the opposition was not enough of an incentive for Defoe, the game would give him another chance to impress the England coaching staff as Tord Grip was again in the directors' box at White Hart Lane. It took just 14 minutes of play for Sven's number two to see that an extended spell out of the team had done little to dampen Defoe's spirit. The striker admitted after the game that he'd had a point to prove, and he did just that as he used his ability on the ball to shimmy and swerve past defender Jonathan Fortune and, with the aid of a deflection, his shot found its way home.

Defoe was partnering Robbie Keane in the Spurs attack, and despite the criticisms that had been levelled at the pairing, they proved their worth in this game. The Ireland international was at the centre of Tottenham's second goal with a pinpoint pass for Jermaine Jenas, who continued his own impressive goalscoring form to double the home side's lead.

Just a minute into the second half the points were safe thanks to Defoe, who stormed on to a through ball from teenage midfielder Tom Huddlestone to get away from the Charlton defence and tuck the ball home for his second goal of the game. It was a reminder to the watching England representative that he still harboured serious ambitions of heading to Germany in the summer. Charlton did get a consolation goal late in the game but Defoe had stolen the show as Tottenham's push for a place among European football's elite took on renewed urgency.

Jol was delighted to see his main striker looking back to his best, and made his feelings clear to the media. 'Jermain is probably the best finisher in England,' he said. 'Hopefully he can improve on his game and has done so in the time that he has not been playing. It's about team building – it's not about Germany or anything. Everyone knows that Jermain and Robbie Keane are great second strikers, but I do favour someone who is really strong to hold the ball up. But I asked Sven-Göran Eriksson recently why he had not played Jermain up front with Michael Owen and he said: "It's difficult; it's the same for everyone." Jermain is too big a player to need to prove a point. He never disappoints me, but it's about balance sometimes. But if he scores goals like that then I will always play him.'

So Defoe had again earned his manager's faith and been rewarded with a place in the team on the most regular basis he had experienced since the early stages of the season. Before the Charlton game he had started just three times in 13 matches. However, a dynamic performance coupled with a pair of well-taken goals was all it needed to prove that he was still one of the hottest properties in the Premier League.

And no matter how many people, including Martin Jol, were saying that he and Keane could not play in the same team, one of the smallest strike partnerships in the division was continuing to silence the critics. Next time it was the Irishman who got on the scoresheet in a 1-1 draw at Sunderland after Defoe had beaten the offside trap in the first half to send over a superb cross that Keane side-footed home with ease.

But Keane would be the one to suffer, being left out for the following home game against Wigan Athletic. Mido came back into the side and equalised after Spurs had fallen behind early on. The home side's performance was not their best of the season and they conceded another goal midway through the second half, only for Defoe to pop up again with his second goal in three games with a neat chipped finish after being set up by the Egyptian. It was the perfect encapsulation of the big man/little man partnership that Jol was so keen on. Not only that, it was yet another demonstration that Defoe could not be ignored when considering who to pick for the Three Lions.

The next England squad to be picked was not for the World Cup but for another friendly, this time against Uruguay at Liverpool's Anfield. Again, Defoe would be in the squad and would feature on match day, but as his club manager had intimated, Sven-Göran Eriksson was still finding it 'difficult' to accommodate the 23-year-old in his strongest team. This time, it was Charlton's striker Darren Bent who partnered Wayne Rooney up front in the absence of Michael Owen. It was tough to take for Defoe, but there was little doubt that Bent deserved his chance after a fantastic season of scoring goals.

However, Bent was unable to make the impact he so desired and was eventually replaced by Defoe with just a few minutes left on the clock. As a result, there would little opportunity for him to shine either. Instead it was Peter Crouch, who had come on for Rooney midway through the second half, who stole the headlines with his first international goal to equalise. Defoe's former West Ham team-mate Joe Cole then sealed the win in the last minute. But for Defoe it was yet another frustrating night in the national shirt, although it did nothing to quench his desire to represent his country.

There would be further frustration as he was left on the bench again for Tottenham. Despite its recent success, Martin Jol had abandoned using the Defoe-Keane partnership following the return of Mido. This time the manager decided to play Keane, and while the England striker would be left kicking his heels for the entire game, Jol's choice was vindicated as two strikes from the Irishman and a winner from the Egyptian gave Tottenham a 3-2 win.

The victory put Spurs five points clear of Arsenal in fourth place and made them strong favourites for the final Champions League place. With the season entering March and just ten Premier League fixtures remaining, their destiny was very much in their own hands. However, Defoe was in little mood for celebrating. He cut an annoyed figure on the bench and at the end of the game he disappeared down the tunnel instead of remaining to celebrate the victory. He could perhaps be forgiven, though – his recent form in a Tottenham shirt had been more than good enough to earn a run in the team.

While Defoe would go on start the majority of the remaining games, another late cameo was all he would be given as Tottenham fell to a morale-crushing defeat with the very last kick of the game against Chelsea at Stamford Bridge. With the game tied at 1-1 going into injury time, defender William Gallas came up with a bolt from the blue to win the game. His stunning strike from outside the area not only boosted his side's title hopes, it threw a spanner into the works of Tottenham's fourth place aspirations. Perhaps with more time on the pitch, Defoe could have helped to have put Spurs into a position where they could have won the game. After all, his record against the big clubs throughout his career had been impressive. However, it was not to be on this occasion.

Defoe returned to the side at St Andrews to help Tottenham get back to winning ways against Birmingham. It would be another dynamic display of what he could offer the team other than goals as he set up the opener with a piece of strength and power that belied his slight frame. He managed to outmuscle Mario Melchiot – a six foot two inch defender – on the left wing and sent over a superb cross to fellow World Cup hopeful Aaron Lennon, who gratefully finished for his first Premier League goal. Before that Defoe could have given his side the lead on more than one occasion but he was twice denied by Northern Ireland goalkeeper Maik Taylor. Instead, it was Robbie Keane who scored late on as Spurs took back the fourth spot that Arsenal had occupied briefly after winning earlier in the day.

Keane's goal convinced the manager to keep him in the side for the following game against West Brom at the Lane, but surprisingly chose Defoe to play alongside him instead of Mido. It proved to be a strange move considering the number of long balls that Tottenham played throughout the game to two strikers who were some way from being target men. However, Keane got two goals to turn the game in the north London club's favour after falling behind in the first half, though not without help from his partner in crime. With the score at 1-1 and the game entering its final minute, Defoe charged down a clearance from Albion keeper Tomasz Kuszczak before the Pole dragged him down to concede a penalty that Keane converted for the winner. Defoe had earlier spurned a decent chance to score, but again he had demonstrated his value to the team's cause.

Unfortunately his lack of goals earned him a total of just half an hour of football in Tottenham's next two games as he came from the bench in the latter stages of a 3-1 defeat at Newcastle and a 2-1 win at home to Manchester City. However, with three wins from their last four games, Spurs were still looking an excellent bet for fourth place. Defoe would return to the side to play a regular part in the team's crucial run in to the end of the season, but with a home game against Manchester United and a make-or-break visit to Arsenal on the horizon, it was not going to be an easy route to Europe.

But first up was a trip to Everton in front of Sven-Göran Eriksson. It was another opportunity for Defoe to show he should be part of the World Cup squad for England, but it was another young Englishman who caught the eye. Right winger Aaron Lennon had an excellent game in front of the England head coach, while Defoe could not make the most of two good chances that came his way early in the second half. Instead the winning goal would again go to Keane. That stretched Defoe's run of appearances without a goal to six, but that did not stop Martin Jol leaping to his defence. He was convinced the young man should be on his way to Germany.

He told the press: 'It makes me laugh when I hear that Jermain Defoe can't go to the World Cup because he lacks rhythm, though he's played five out of seven games for us. Michael Owen is not playing and he'll go to Germany for sure.' It seemed a fair point as Owen had been suffering with injuries for much of the season, but there was little doubt the Newcastle striker's pedigree was enough to warrant a place among the England party.

Another man expecting to feature up front for England

would upstage Defoe in the next game. Wayne Rooney ensured Manchester United left White Hart Lane with all three points in a game that the Defoe and Keane could do little to influence as they were stifled by another England and Ireland double act in Rio Ferdinand and John O'Shea. Mido was injured and there was little doubt that the front two were in desperate need of a physical presence against such a resolute defence. The defeat piled the pressure on Tottenham ahead of their visit to Arsenal in what would be the final north London derby at the old Highbury stadium.

Again Defoe struggled. This was the most important game in Tottenham's season but a combination of a lack of support and the traditional tight nature of such a crucial derby, plus the huge pressure on all the players involved, meant that he was unable to make the impact on the game he so badly wanted.

In a bad-tempered affair, Keane gave Spurs the lead in controversial circumstances. With Arsenal players Emmanuel Eboue and Gilberto Silva down injured, Tottenham continued to attack. The ball eventually found its way to the Irishman who prodded home to spark a heated confrontation on the touchline between Jol and his Gunners counterpart Arsène Wenger, who felt Spurs should have put the ball out of play.

However, the introduction of Arsenal's French talisman Thierry Henry from the bench changed the game. His stunning equaliser earned a point for the hosts in a game that, in truth, they rarely looked like getting anything out of. Tottenham remained ahead of Arsenal after the draw, but the intriguing subplot to the situation was that the Gunners were due to play in the Champions League final against Barcelona. Should they win, then it would not matter where Tottenham finished in the table. As holders, Arsenal would automatically qualify as the fourth English team.

All Tottenham could do was concentrate on their own progress. They could have no say in what Arsenal would do in Paris, but they could ensure they won their own games. Against Bolton at White Hart Lane they did that, but again Defoe could not get on the scoresheet. That made it ten games without a goal and another goalless appearance in front of the England manager. It was all the more frustrating given that Wayne Rooney had broken a metatarsal bone in his foot the previous day and was a major doubt for the World Cup. It was a serious chance for Defoe to force his way into the squad but again luck was not on his side. He was subbed after 77 minutes.

But Defoe knew the most important thing was the last game of the season. Of all the teams that Spurs had to beat to reach the Champions League, of all the teams Defoe could face in the most important club game of his career, it was West Ham at Upton Park. It turned into one of the most unpredictable days in the history of the Premier League.

There was nothing unpredictable about the fact it was a closely fought London derby. There was nothing unpredictable about the abuse that Defoe would have to take from the Hammer support. There was nothing unpredictable about him scoring against his old club on his old home ground. The element of the unpredictable came the night before the game, at the hotel in which Tottenham had stayed.

No fewer than six, and some newspapers reported ten, members of the Tottenham squad were hit by a bug after eating what was believed to be a lasagne meal. It was the worst possible preparation for the biggest game of their season. Manager Martin Jol tried desperately to get the game delayed after being alerted by the team doctor on match day, but it was to little avail. Spurs would have to play – ill or not.

What had looked like being a dream season for Tottenham had turned into an absolute horror story. Defoe scored an excellent equaliser after they went a goal down with a neat touch past Anton Ferdinand and a quality finish. It was his ninth goal of the season, but it was not going to be enough. Israeli midfielder Yossi Benayoun ensured Tottenham's season would end in devastation rather than celebration with the winning goal. While Spurs mourned the death of their Champions League hopes, the red-and-white half of north London rejoiced as a 4-2 win against Wigan in Highbury's last ever game guaranteed them a place in European football's club showpiece, regardless of what happened against Barcelona – a game they went on to lose. Normally a season including a place in the UEFA Cup and Arsenal losing a major final would be deemed a successful one for Spurs. But this one felt like failure. And for Defoe, it was all about to get a lot worse.

The end of the season brought about the announcement of England's squad for the World Cup in Germany. There had been plenty of speculation over who Sven-Göran Eriksson would take as his strikers. Wayne Rooney was still a doubt, Michael Owen had not played a full season, and strikers like Peter Crouch and Darren Bent were competing with Defoe for a place on the plane. But no one could have predicted what happened next.

Eriksson decided to name Rooney in the squad, despite his injury, in the hope that he would make a full recovery in time for the start of the tournament. Not surprisingly Michael Owen was also selected; his experience and international goalscoring record made him a certainty for selection. The third spot went to Peter Crouch. While many questioned his international credentials, his six feet seven inch frame would be sure to cause problems for defenders. But when the fourth name was read out, the amazement was palpable.

The selection of Arsenal teenager Theo Walcott for the England World Cup squad sent shockwaves throughout English football. At just 17 years of age, the January signing from Southampton had not even played a first-team game for Arsenal. He had still to play for England's under-21s. Yet here he was, selected to represent the country in the biggest tournament of them all, ahead of the top English goalscorer in the Premier League – Bent – and a man who had been a part of every England squad in qualifying all season – Defoe.

Bent was omitted altogether, but Defoe was named as one of five standby players in case Rooney was not able to overcome his foot injury in time. There was still hope that the Tottenham man could make it to the finals, and many believed he deserved a place there. However, in a very short space of time that hope would turn to despair.

Chapter 7

End Of The World

Standby status would be a strange experience for Defoe. He had effectively been put in a position whereby he would be heavily involved in all of England's build-up to the World Cup – all the preparation, friendly matches and training sessions – but he was unlikely to play any part in the actual competition. Wayne Rooney was back in Manchester going through extensive treatment, including the use of an oxygen tent, in the hope he would be able to travel to Germany. It was a turbulent time for Defoe. On the one hand he would never wish ill on a team-mate and wanted England to have the best possible chance of winning the World Cup. On the other, he was desperate to play a part.

He was given something of an opportunity with 12 minutes of action in an England 'B' international against Belarus after coming on as a substitute for Peter Crouch. Theo Walcott was given half an hour to prove to the nation he was ready for the national team, but while he did himself no harm, it was clear he would be nothing more than an impact sub who could trouble opponents with his searing pace. There was still little evidence to suggest he should have been afforded a place in the squad ahead of Defoe. Indeed England's surprise 2-1 defeat led to more than a few questions about their World Cup prospects.

Walcott would get another run-out against Hungary at Old Trafford before sitting out the final pre-World Cup friendly, against Jamaica at the same ground. England won both games, 3-1 and 6-0 respectively, with Michael Owen and Crouch showing their goalscoring credentials. It was heart-rending for Defoe to watch the strikers he had competed so valiantly against, and indeed played alongside, enjoying being among the goals in the full knowledge they would be performing on the big stage. At that point, he still knew nothing of his fate.

That would come soon enough. Having travelled to Germany with the squad after being involved with them for a month, Defoe learned that Rooney had finally been passed fit to join the England party. Sven-Göran Eriksson invited Defoe to stay with the squad, but it was no surprise when he elected to get back home as quickly as possible. To have been involved for so long before being told he was not needed after all was too much for the young striker.

It seemed that nobody could quite believe Defoe would not be part of the World Cup finals. Many people in the game including current players, ex-players and journalists could not understand why he had been omitted from the squad. Liverpool captain and England midfielder Steven Gerrard was one of the first to praise Defoe for his attitude while with the squad. 'Jermain has been really professional,' he said. 'He's shown a great attitude and it's a shame for him because he's such a wonderful talent. The players are really sad to see him go but unfortunately the manager can only pick 23 players.' It was a point Gerrard would follow-up in his post-World Cup autobiography, in which he criticised Eriksson's decision to take Walcott to Germany.

Indeed it was almost impossible to understand Eriksson's decision to omit Defoe. This was in no way a criticism of Walcott – the decision was nothing to do with him – but simply a question of why a player who had been a squad regular was suddenly left behind in favour of a player who yet to begin to make his mark on the international scene. The coach was due to stand down at the end of the World Cup. Perhaps he wanted to go out with a memorable gamble that would have ensured legendary status had it paid off. Perhaps he'd simply had a hunch that such an unknown quantity would come up trumps. He even admitted it was something of a last-minute decision. But whatever the reason, 'one of the best strikers in Europe', according to England captain David Beckham, would not be going to Germany.

Unsurprisingly, Martin Jol leapt to the defence of his star. He was hoping Defoe would be part of a strong Tottenham contingent in the England squad, including Paul Robinson, Michael Carrick, Aaron Lennon and Jermaine Jenas. 'I think he (Eriksson) has made a mistake,' the Spurs boss told BBC Radio 5 Live, citing the problem England had of having only two recognised strikers and an injured Rooney on board.

As for Defoe, he just could not get his head around why he was back at home. In an emotional interview with the *News of the World* he said, 'I don't know why I'm not out there. I've been involved in every squad for the last two years and feel

I've played a part in helping us to qualify. I have never felt fitter and sharper than I was in training and believe I could have scored goals in the tournament. It's a strange decision and everyone I speak to thinks so as well.'

And so it proved. England negotiated the group stages having made hard work of their victories against Paraguay and Trinidad & Tobago, but things started to go wrong in their 2-2 draw with Sweden. With just three minutes gone, Michael Owen collapsed in agony and was stretchered off with a serious knee injury. Not only would he miss the end of the tournament, he would be out for much of the following season. Rooney was making his first start in the competition as he continued his recovery, and in an instant it became abundantly clear that England could have done with Defoe.

Another workmanlike performance saw off Ecuador in the first knockout round thanks to a Beckham free-kick, but England's lack of options up front was beginning to show. The point was hammered home against Portugal in the quarter-final. England could only draw 0-0 after Rooney was sent off for a stamp on Chelsea defender Ricardo Carvalho. They then lost on penalties. It was another agonising World Cup experience for England, another heroic failure.

In Eriksson's final press conference as England manager he was interrogated by the media about why he had not taken another striker – namely Defoe. Wouldn't the Tottenham striker have been a more sensible option than Walcott, especially given the circumstances? 'I don't think so,' said the outgoing coach. 'If I had thought so I would have picked him.' He later added: 'Jermain had a very bad season. I don't think he deserved to go to the World Cup. Taking Theo was the right decision. Where are the other good English forwards? I saw 100, 120 Premiership games every year and I couldn't find out.' Defoe had scored nine times, while Darren Bent had been the division's top English goalscorer. There was little doubt they were both 'good English forwards'.

So once again it would be up to Defoe to prove his doubters wrong. With Eriksson on his way, it was time to impress another manager – Eriksson's number two Steve McLaren, who was set to take the reins. While the circumstances were less than favourable for Defoe, the situation was nothing he was not used to. Yes, the spring had turned into a disaster for Spurs and the summer had only made things worse. But there were positives: the England coach who did not want him had gone, Tottenham had enjoyed their best ever season in the Premier League and, for the first time in his career, Defoe would get the chance to play European club football. It was time for a fresh start.

Before the 2006/07 season kicked off, there was an England friendly to be played at Old Trafford against Greece – the first match under the new manager. While most of the talk before the game had been about McLaren's omission of former captain David Beckham from the squad, one selection almost went unnoticed. With both Michael Owen and Wayne Rooney injured, a place in the side from the start went to Defoe. It was a remarkable turnaround following the summer he had just been through, although four goals in pre-season with Tottenham had shown his eye for goal was still very much intact.

He and England would not disappoint the crowd of more than 40,000 who came to witness the dawning of the latest England era. After the new skipper John Terry had headed the home side into the lead, Defoe was on hand to play a part in the second goal of the game with a perfect pass to Frank Lampard, whose deflected effort doubled England's advantage. Two more goals from Peter Crouch wrapped up a comfortable win for England, and another was to follow.

Despite failing to find the net in Tottenham's first three games of the season, Defoe retained his place in the England team for the opening qualifiers of England's 2008 European Championship campaign, starting with a home match against minnows Andorra. It was a great opportunity for Defoe to score his first England goal since his single strike in Poland two years before. It was an opportunity he would grab with both hands.

First he was involved in the build-up to the opening goal, scored by Crouch, before Steven Gerrard swept in a second. Then Defoe reminded the nation of what they might have seen in Germany had things been different. Seven minutes before half-time he made an instinctive, darting run to the near post to hit a beautifully controlled left-footed volley into the net. Two minutes after the interval he netted number four from close range. Crouch added a fifth in the second half as this developing strike partnership again impressed.

Defoe was delighted to be back in the England fold under a manager who clearly wanted him in the squad. The striker made his feelings clear after the game with praise for McLaren, and perhaps a thinly veiled criticism of the previous England coach who had so cruelly snubbed him. He said: 'The manager has been fantastic to me. He is a great coach. This week's training has been great and to be back in the team is great.' Missing out on the World Cup had clearly hurt and he was relishing the chance of a new beginning.

'It's hard to put into words what it felt like when the squad was announced and I wasn't in it,' he added. 'It was soul-destroying. I was part of the squad for two years and then I wasn't there. It was so hard to get left behind. It was a massive disappointment to miss out on the World Cup, but scoring these goals makes up for it in some way. When you get disappointments in your career it makes you stronger and I suppose you want to prove people wrong and work even harder. I've done that and I'm getting my rewards now.'

McLaren also spoke of his delight at the performances of Defoe and Crouch, and decided to keep the pair together up front for the following qualifier in Macedonia. England made hard work of it but Crouch scored the only goal of the game to maintain the new coach's 100 per cent start at the helm. The closest Defoe came was with an acrobatic overhead kick that dropped wide, but it was clear McLaren was determined to give him the kind of run in the national team that many felt he deserved.

But back at White Hart Lane, Defoe was once again enduring something of a topsy-turvy time. Having started in an opening day defeat at Bolton, he was on the bench for the next two games – a home win over newly promoted Sheffield United and a home defeat by Everton. His two England goals at Old Trafford would not earn him a start for his next visit there against Manchester United, with Spurs falling to their third defeat in four games.

It had not been an easy start to Tottenham's season. Martin Jol had lost a number of players, including central midfield duo Michael Carrick and Andy Reid. In addition, several new players had been signed. Steed Malbranque and Pascal Chimbonda had joined from Fulham and Wigan respectively, and the manager had also brought in talent from abroad with the likes of Benoit Assou-Ekotto and Didier Zokora leaving the French league to come to England. Perhaps the biggest signing of all was talented Bulgarian striker Dimitar Berbatov from Germany. However, while there was no shortage of talent on show, it was taking a while for Jol's new team to gel.

The new-look Tottenham would be given another stern early-season test as they began their UEFA Cup campaign. A two-legged tie against Czech outfit Slavia Prague gave them the opportunity to reach the group stages of the competition, and after failing to reach the Champions League, Jol's charges were desperate not to waste this opportunity to play in Europe. Defoe was a constant thorn in Slavia's side with his quick and inventive running, and caused them no shortage of problems in only his second start of the season. However, the only goal of the game went to Jermaine Jenas – it was Tottenham's first away goal in Europe for 15 years. Defoe would not feature in the second leg, but another 1-0 win was enough to take the club into the main competition.

Goals were proving hard to come by for Defoe, as he fired blanks in a goalless draw at home to Fulham and a 3-0 hammering at Liverpool. His first league goal of the season finally came in early October, against Portsmouth at White Hart Lane. Spurs were already a goal to the good when summer signing Zokora went down very easily in the area. As Pompey fumed, a penalty was given and up stepped Defoe to calmly place the ball beyond former team-mate David James' reach to put Tottenham on their way to only their second Premier League win of the season.

Unfortunately Spurs would not get the chance to build quickly on their success as another international break was coming up. Defoe would be involved again, but this time in a disappointing couple of games that were to have huge implications for England's Euro 2008 qualification attempt. Wayne Rooney returned to the team to play Macedonia at home, but his failure to find the net prompted McLaren to replace him with Defoe in the second half. 'I took Wayne off because I was just trying to win a football match,' the manager said afterwards. The game finished 0-0, but it was another display of his trust in Defoe.

But it was not enough to earn Defoe a start for the trip to Croatia that would prove disastrous for England. McLaren decided to use a previously untested 3-5-2 formation but his team crashed to a dismal 2-0 defeat, thanks in part to a howler from keeper Paul Robinson, who inexplicably allowed a Gary Neville backpass to bobble under his foot and into the net. Defoe was thrown on for the last 15 minutes but it was too little too late.

Early season it may have been, but again an element of frustration was creeping into Defoe's game. His first goal of the season for Spurs had not helped him keep his place for England, Tottenham were not winning games on anything like a regular basis and as a result the goals would disappear again for the next three games. First up was a Premier League draw against Aston Villa, followed by a first UEFA Cup group-stage win over Besiktas in Turkey, in which he would only play a minute. By the time the third game came around, against West Ham at the Lane, he had reached boiling point.

While Mido scored the winning goal, the match was remembered for a 42nd-minute flare-up after Defoe had been fouled from behind by Argentinean midfielder Javier Mascherano. The two squared up and the England striker appeared to bite Mascherano on the shoulder. Both players were booked but had referee Steve Bennett seen more, it might well have been worse for Defoe. Martin Jol tried to laugh off the incident but later intimated he had disciplined Defoe internally. Mascherano described the affair as 'the worst thing I've been involved in since I've been in England' but Defoe insisted it was a one-off.

'That definitely won't happen again,' he told the *Evening Standard*. 'It was out of character. I don't know how many bookings I got last season or the season before but I don't usually get involved like that. I don't go out there to hurt people. I just want to play football and score goals.' Nevertheless the incident showed Defoe in a very poor light and proved he still had a way to go before his temperament was problem-free.

Defoe and Tottenham were both in need of a boost, and a League Cup tie at Milton Keynes Dons was to provide them with just that. Defoe scored twice to set Tottenham on the way to a crushing 5-0 victory. His first goal made it 2-0 as he collected Mido's pass and lifted the ball over the advancing goalkeeper. It was a landmark strike – his 100th in professional club football – and it was followed by another smart finish minutes later. Dons manager Martin Allen, a former Hammer, couldn't resist a joke: 'Defoe certainly had some bite tonight. He sank his teeth into us.'

The League Cup would turn into a season-saving competition for Jermain Defoe. Berbatov was beginning to strike up a strong partnership with Robbie Keane as manager Jol again made clear his intention not to play the Irishman and Englishman together. Defoe would be forced to sit out another win in Europe, this time against Club Brugge from Belgium,

Defoe in action for Spurs. He left the club for Portsmouth in 2008 but would return to White Hart Lane just a year later.

Little and large: Jermain Defoe and Peter Crouch were team-mates at Portsmouth and both followed Harry Redknapp to Spurs in 2009.

Above: Defoe tussles with Nemanja Vidic in December 2009. He enjoyed a fantastic season with Spurs in 2009/10 which culminated in a top-four Premier League finish.

Below: Making his World Cup finals debut against Algeria on 18 June 2010.

Defoe scoring his first World Cup goal, against Slovenia in England's final group stage match.

Happy times in Port Elizabeth as Defoe's strike gives England the victory they needed to progress to the knockout stages.

Above: Defoe relaxing at England's World Cup base camp in Rustenburg.

Below: Lining up with the team ahead of their Round of 16 clash with Germany on 27 June.

Defoe in action against Germany.

Sadly England's World Cup fell short of expectations as the side suffered a 4-1 defeat to Germany. But Defoe's performance was one of the positive things to come out of the tournament and he is surely set for great things in years to come.

before getting just six minutes of a fantastic 2-1 win at home to Chelsea. Many players would be irritated at missing so many big games, and perhaps Defoe was, but he certainly did not show it.

He returned to the starting line-up to play Port Vale in the next round of the League Cup. While Spurs made hard work of it, Defoe netted the winner in extra time with a swept finish from young defender Phil Ifil's cross, sending Tottenham into the quarter-finals with a 3-1 victory. It was also a goal that would start a turnaround in his fortunes with a run of nine goals in nine starts.

After a substitute appearance in a defeat against Reading and a stint on the bench for England's 1-1 friendly draw in Holland, Defoe made his first league start since the bad-tempered encounter against West Ham in a visit to Blackburn Rovers. After Tugay had given the hosts the lead, the Turkish midfielder was sent off for bringing down Hossam Ghaly in the box, allowing Defoe to send his penalty just about beyond the reach of keeper Brad Friedel and ensure a point for his team.

While he would miss the next European tie against Bayer Leverkusen, in which Berbatov would score the only goal of the game against his former club, Defoe would be back in the side to face Wigan at White Hart Lane. While Keane and Berbatov had earned the early season plaudits, it looked like Defoe's partnership with the gangling Bulgarian was worth persevering with. The two combined effectively as Defoe reached another landmark, finishing off Berbatov's pass for his 50th Premier League goal – the opener in a 3-1 win.

Despite not starting in Tottenham's 3-0 defeat at local rivals Arsenal, Defoe would go on to start every one of his next ten appearances. A home win against Middlesbrough was followed by a 5-1 thrashing of Charlton, in which Defoe scored the goal of the game with a dipping long-range effort. Finally, Defoe would get his chance in the UEFA Cup group stage with two goals against Dinamo Bucharest as Spurs won 3-1. The first goal was a compelling reminder of just how good he was, collecting the ball ten yards inside the Dinamo half before setting off on a fantastic run through the defence and ending with a lethal strike.

All of a sudden, Tottenham's season had turned around. With five wins from their last six games they were looking like a side that was ready to compete at the right end of the Premier League, and it was no surprise that their change in fortunes going hand in hand with Defoe's improved form. His fine run in the Carling Cup continued with the only goal, again in extra time, against Southend to steer Spurs to the semi-finals and a meeting with Arsenal.

Next it became a Christmas to remember for Defoe and Spurs as he scored two more goals in a 2-1 home win against Aston Villa on Boxing Day. For both goals he combined expertly with Berbatov to steer the team to their 12th straight home win, to the delight of the manager. Jol told the media after the game: 'Jermain was the difference today. It's as simple as that. He has been our sharpest forward this season.' He had come a long way from his quiet start.

The partnership between Defoe and Berbatov was gathering momentum, leading Defoe to hint to his manager that the two of them be given the chance to blossom as 2007 arrived. 'We've got an understanding now and it just keeps getting better,' he said. 'And obviously the more we play together the better it will get.' He was beginning to enjoy his football again and made it clear to the media how happy he was to be back in the team and back among the goals. He was also being noticed by other Premier League managers, not least Portsmouth boss Harry Redknapp – the man who had brought him to West Ham. 'He needs to play regularly,' he told the *Daily Mail*. 'If he was here he'd be a superstar. He'd play every week in my team.' But Redknapp would have to wait a while for that.

Defoe lined up against Portsmouth on New Year's Day but 2007 would get off to slow start for him. Two days earlier he could not make the desired impact in a 2-0 home defeat by Liverpool, and again he would fail to score as Spurs came away from the south coast with a 1-1 draw. He would suffer another quiet day in the third round of the FA Cup at Cardiff City, but as was so often the case with Defoe the goals were not too far away.

Newcastle were the visitors to White Hart Lane on a brisk mid-January afternoon and they were subjected to an early onslaught. In front of the England manager, Defoe made sure he continued to impress. After seeing an early effort brilliantly saved by Ireland keeper Shay Given, he continued to pressurise the Magpies defence before reaching Steed Malbranque's cross before anyone else to net his 13th goal of the season. A quick equaliser early in the second half was forgotten about when Berbatov restored Tottenham's lead, but a late collapse ruined all their hard work when first Nicky Butt and then a superb strike from Obafemi Martins stunned the Lane.

Martin Jol was in need of a distraction as that defeat looked set to ruin his upcoming 51st birthday. Fortunately that distraction would come with Tottenham's replay against Cardiff back at home. They cruised to a 4-0 win and after coming on as a substitute for Berbatov, Defoe scored his fifth goal in seven games, capitalising on the Championship side's failure to clear their lines and lashing home the final goal of the game.

While Spurs had improved their Premier League form and still looked like they could get into Europe again (albeit not in the top four), it was becoming clear that the domestic cups were their best chance of silverware. That they were struggling to pick up wins in the league was demonstrated by another draw – their second in three games and their fourth match without a win – this time against Fulham at Craven Cottage.

This made their League Cup semi-final tie with Arsenal even more important than it would normally be. A north London derby is always a crucial affair, but with a place in a major final at Cardiff's Millennium Stadium at stake as well, the meeting would go down as one of the biggest in recent history.

Having supported the Gunners as a child, Defoe was always desperate to do well against them and he was a menace throughout the 80 minutes he played in the first leg at White Hart Lane. After threatening to open the scoring early on, he sent over an excellent cross from the right that allowed his partner Berbatov to open the scoring from close range. It was a nice move between two players showing that together they could deliver goals. However, the introduction of Arsenal's on-loan Brazilian Julio Baptista had a profound effect. After deflecting in a free-kick to put his side two goals down, the man known as 'The Beast' took it upon himself to make amends, and his two goals swung the semi-final in Arsenal's favour as they headed back to their new Emirates Stadium with the score at 2-2.

Tottenham's focus on cup football would continue, with

their next FA Cup engagement sandwiched in between the two League Cup games. Defoe was a late substitute as his team cruised to a 3-1 home win against Southend, but he could not score the winner against them as he had done earlier in the season. However, the bigger game was to follow. Spurs were 90 minutes from Cardiff as they faced their near neighbours once more.

In the absence of Berbatov, Jol's choice of strikers raised a few eyebrows. As Russell Kempson explained in *The Times*: 'Mysterious, too, was the lack of Jol's preferred little-and-large combination up front. Instead of Mido with Robbie Keane or Jermain Defoe, he went for the small-and-smaller combination of Keane and Defoe. Stranger and stranger.' And so it proved. Mido later came off the bench to keep Spurs in the tie with a late equaliser after Emmanuel Adebayor had put Arsenal ahead. But it was to no avail as an extra-time goal from Jeremie Aliadiere and an own goal by Pascal Chimbonda sent Arsenal through. It was a gutting experience for Spurs and their supporters to have come so close to beating their fiercest rivals to the final, and it was particularly galling for Defoe, who so badly wanted to impress against the team he had followed growing up.

It was to be another difficult spell for Defoe. He played only 55 minutes of Tottenham's next game – a 4-0 mauling in front of their own fans at the hands of title-chasing Manchester United – before he made a brief appearance from the bench for England in a 1-0 friendly defeat by Spain, which ended in the national team being booed off the pitch at Old Trafford. His dip in form had not gone unnoticed by Martin Jol, who opted to play Keane and Berbatov for the next three matches. It worked in two of them as a defeat at Sheffield United was followed by back-to-back wins against Everton and Bolton – games in which both strikers would find the net.

But Jol was keen to keep his strikers happy. He had made it clear to all of them that he would be doing his best to rotate the squad as much as possible without harming the team, so it was no surprise to see Defoe return to the starting line-up quickly. Jol was no fool and realised that if there was one game that Defoe wanted to be involved with from the start, it was an away fixture at West Ham. He was booed, jeered and abused for all 90 minutes of the game, but he would have the last laugh on a fantastic day for Spurs.

Spurs went two goals down in the first half, but Lee Bowyer tripped Aaron Lennon in the box and up stepped Defoe to take the penalty. The noise was deafening but the 24-year-old showed great maturity and composure to slot the ball coolly past goalkeeper Robert Green and bring Spurs back into the game. An equaliser from Teemu Tainio was followed by the Hammers taking the lead again through Bobby Zamora – the man with whom Defoe had swapped places three years earlier – but Berbatov levelled in the last minute. And there was more to come.

Defoe was not content to see the game finish in a draw. He was desperate to put in a performance in front of the fans who had continued to give him such a hard time. Deep into injury time he set off on a blistering 60-yard run before letting fly with a low strike that Green did well to keep out. However, the shot was too hot to handle and Paul Stalteri was on hand right in front of goal to tap home the winner. It was the first time Tottenham had led in the game and it earned them a massive three points in their quest for European football.

Spurs were next in action in Europe, although Defoe would

be the unfortunate striker to miss out as part of the manager's rotation policy. There was no doubt that Jol wanted to keep all his players as fresh as possible with progress in the UEFA Cup, FA Cup and Premier League all still possible with only a couple of months left in the season.

Defoe did not feature in Tottenham's 3-2 win at Portuguese club Braga in the last 16 of the UEFA Cup, but he returned to the team for a huge FA Cup game against Chelsea at Stamford Bridge. Defoe could not get himself a goal but he more than played his part in a pulsating affair that Tottenham should have come away from victorious. First he combined beautifully with Aaron Lennon to set up Berbatov, who hammered them into the lead. Frank Lampard levelled but two more goals before half-time gave the visitors a seemingly unassailable two-goal advantage. However, Chelsea were one of the best teams in the country for a reason and, despite leaving it until the last 20 minutes, they forced the tie into a replay with two late goals.

Fortunately, Spurs would not have long to dwell on their disappointment as the second leg of their game against Braga would give them the opportunity to reach the quarter-finals of the UEFA Cup. Defoe only entered the game with 25 minutes left on the clock and was again goalless, but he knew that did not matter as the team's 3-2 victory sent them into the last eight of the competition. He was fully aware of the extent of this achievement, and despite not having been a regular on their European charge, his efforts earlier in the competition had been as important as anybody's.

Of less consolation for Defoe, however, was that he would only start in one of Tottenham's next four games. He played all 90 minutes of the team's 3-1 win at home to Watford but would not score. Even if he had done, however, it would have probably been forgotten in a game remembered for Spurs keeper Paul Robinson getting himself on the scoresheet with an outrageous clearance from inside his own half that sailed over his England rival Ben Foster and into the net.

Subsequently, Defoe would be restricted to appearances from the bench for both club and country. He struggled to get involved in the FA Cup replay against Chelsea, despite being given the best part of half an hour as Spurs crashed out, before playing just 15 minutes of Tottenham's win against Reading. He did not even get on the pitch for the first leg of the UEFA Cup quarter-final against Sevilla in Spain, a game Spurs lost 2-1.

It was a similarly frustrating period in England colours. With both Peter Crouch and Michael Owen unavailable for the European Championship qualifier against Israel in Tel Aviv, Defoe might have expected to be given a game. However, Steve McLaren opted for Everton striker Andy Johnson to partner Wayne Rooney up front. The game finished 0-0, and in the ten minutes Defoe was given as a replacement for Johnson he had the best chance of the game, forcing the Israeli goalkeeper into a good stop. How different things could have been had he been allowed to play the entire match.

England under McLaren were making hard work of qualifying for Euro 2008, and faced suffering the most humiliating of results when they went in goalless at half-time against Andorra in Barcelona. Again, Defoe was left out of the side, and again he would provide a much-needed spark when he did enter the fray. After Steven Gerrard had finally given England a lead they barely deserved, he and Defoe neatly exchanged passes before adding his second with a low strike.

Defoe would make the third and final goal of the night as well when his low shot was only half-stopped by the goalkeeper and was rolling over the line when debutant David Nugent made sure by tapping the ball in.

Defoe's only start in April would come in Tottenham's single-goal defeat by Chelsea as the month turned into a disappointing one for him. He came off the bench to score with his first touch in the UEFA Cup second leg against Sevilla at White Hart Lane, but Spurs could only manage a 2-2 draw and their hopes of silverware were dashed for another year. Jol seemed to have finally decided that Keane and Berbatov was the strike partnership to finish the season with. It proved a sound decision from the team's point of view as the pair would score nine goals in April to earn them the rare accolade of joint-Player of the Month in the Premier League. With those two in such scintillating form, it was never going to be easy for Defoe to get his place back, especially with so few games left in the season.

One defeat in their past nine Premier League games had put Tottenham on the brink of qualifying for the UEFA Cup again and with three matches remaining they were favourites to grab the all-important fifth place for the second season running. Despite his diminished presence in the side, Defoe would help his team over the line as the campaign drew to a close. Once again he would score at his old Charlton home to ensure three more points, but his 25-yard effort was bittersweet as it relegated the club where he had grown up. While the fans there gave him plenty of stick, he still had friends at the Valley and he felt sorry for them.

The goal against Charlton earned him plenty of praise from Martin Jol. He appreciated how tough it had been for the striker to only play a peripheral role in the closing stages of the season and gave him a vote of confidence in the press. 'Jermain has a big role – he's playing an important role now,' he said. 'For a player like him it's awful to come off the bench for the last ten minutes. He hates it. But he showed against Charlton he is a fine character.'

He added: 'Other players who I won't mention would make a decision for themselves but he is a team player and knows he has played such a big part this season. Jermain never moans and sometimes I wonder why! He has a great attitude and always wants to show us what he can do. He has so much confidence and when he comes on, he wants to show he could do the business.'

Defoe repaid his manager's faith with a strong performance from the start against Blackburn at White Hart Lane, resulting in a second-half equaliser to keep the European charge going into the final game of the season. Keeper Brad Friedel parried the ball out to him and from close range there was only going to be one outcome. Tottenham still needed to win on the final day of the season at Manchester City, but they did just that to book their place in Europe for their second season in a row.

Defoe finished the season with an impressive 18 goals in all competitions for Tottenham, and was rewarded with a place in the England squad for the summer fixtures, which included a friendly against Brazil in the first international match at the newly redeveloped Wembley Stadium. However, Defoe would be left on the bench for this game, which ended 1-1, and the following 3-0 European Championship qualifying victory over Estonia in Tallinn.

It was quiet break between seasons for Defoe, but at least

this time he had been able to play a more active role with the national team than he had the previous year. However, it was time to focus on the next season with Tottenham. Back in Europe and back in the higher echelons of the Premier League table, Spurs were determined to build on their recent success and try to break into the top four.

With three impressive strikers in Defoe, Berbatov and Keane, Martin Jol knew he had a squad worthy of competing at the top of the division. In fact, in an interview with the official club magazine, Jol claimed that the front three were the most exciting players he had worked with. However, that did not help to dampen speculation about Defoe's future when Tottenham shelled out a whopping £16.5 million to sign fellow England hopeful Darren Bent from relegated Charlton. With four international strikers in the squad, Jol would have an even tougher job keeping everyone happy than he had done the previous season when both Keane and Defoe had to endure lengthy spells on the bench.

Although talk of Defoe wanting to leave the club was rife, he maintained that he was willing to stay and fight for his place. 'I'm really excited about the new season and the prospect of another campaign in Europe,' he told the media. 'We have made some good signings and are now stronger and better equipped to compete in all competitions. We have competition for places in all positions and that can only be good for the team.'

But while Defoe was certainly saying all the right things, he knew it would be a big ask to hold down a regular first-team place. Berbatov and Keane had finished last season as the manager's preferred pairing and Bent was expected to play after coming to the club with such a hefty price tag. There was already reported interest in Defoe from Aston Villa and Portsmouth should he slip down the pecking order – and the latter's manager Harry Redknapp had made no secret of his desire to manage Defoe again after nurturing him at West Ham.

That slip down the pecking order appeared to take place straight away as Defoe would not start a game for Spurs until late September. In the opening games of the season the manager would rotate Berbatov, Keane and Bent – he even started all three in one game – with Defoe left to make his appearances from the bench. It was to prove a difficult start to the season for Tottenham, who lost their opening two games in front of the live television cameras. First they were beaten by Michael Chopra's last-gasp goal for newly promoted Sunderland, before being humbled 3-1 at home by Everton. Their first win of the season came with a comfortable result against Derby but another defeat at Manchester United made it three defeats in four games. Defoe would only play 75 minutes in all those fixtures combined.

His lack of first-team action naturally filtered through to the national set-up and he missed out on three more opportunities to play at the new Wembley. In a friendly against Germany he was left on the bench while Michael Owen played up front alongside his new partner, Newcastle striker Alan Smith. Peter Crouch got a chance to play but Defoe did not in a 2-1 defeat. It was a similar story in the qualifiers that followed as England put themselves back in the driving seat for European Championship qualification with consecutive 3-0 wins against Israel and Russia, again without needing to use Defoe.

The return from international inaction seemed to spur Defoe on as Tottenham began their UEFA Cup campaign with a home game against Cypriot side Anorthosis Famagusta.

When he came off the substitutes' bench in the 63rd minute he was greeted by a rapturous ovation from the White Hart Lane fans, and he repaid them in the best way he knew. Two minutes after coming on, he picked up the ball on the edge of the area and delivered a delightful chip over the goalkeeper. At the end of the game he added a second with a spectacular curling effort that found the top corner and left the keeper standing. His part in a 6-1 victory was a clear reminder to the manager that he could help the faltering team get back to winning ways.

He was rewarded with his first start of the season, albeit in a League Cup tie at home to Middlesbrough. Defoe performed well, creating chances for himself and laying them on for his team-mates in his all-action manner. However, without a goal to his name, he was eventually replaced by Robbie Keane to his obvious disappointment. The move worked, though, as Keane's presence helped the team to a 2-0 victory, and Jol was not best pleased with Defoe's reaction to being substituted. 'He's a human being,' he said. 'Even with children, if they have a lot of support they feel confident. I always say if you come off, you have to show respect for your team-mates.'

While Defoe was understandably irritated, Jol was under pressure. Spurs had still only managed one league win and he seemed unclear as to what his best starting line-up was. He would leave Defoe out until the second half of a 4-4 draw against Aston Villa, a game in which Spurs recovered from 4-1 down. Defoe was involved in Tottenham's comeback as his strike off the post was rebounded in by Pascal Chimbonda. He would get another start in the second leg of the Famagusta tie but would fail to score against the Cypriots in a 1-1 draw which saw Spurs into the group stage of the UEFA Cup.

Defoe started the first group game against Getafe at White Hart Lane, but in the meantime a lot had changed for both club and country. For country, he did not feature as England lost in Russia in a game that could have seen them qualify for the European Championships had they won. It put England back on the brink of disaster with chances to clinch their place in Austria and Switzerland running out fast. For club, the inevitable happened – Martin Jol reached an agreement with the Tottenham board to leave the club, to be replaced by Spanish coach Juande Ramos.

The decision was made shortly before the Getafe game kicked off and led to an eerie atmosphere around the Lane as Spurs fell to a 2-1 defeat. Defoe had given them the lead with his third goal of the season after Berbatov had set him up to glance home a 19th-minute header. The two men had not enjoyed much game time together this season, but they showed they still possessed an impressive understanding. However, it was not to be Tottenham's night and the Jol era ended in disappointment.

Despite the change in management it would still prove difficult for Defoe to nail down a place in the Tottenham team. His first start since Jol's departure did not come until early November in a draw at Middlesbrough, but his decent form from the bench allowed him to keep his place in the England squad. Despite his lack of recent goals, Steve McLaren knew he needed Defoe as part of his armoury for the make-or-break qualifier against Croatia.

Before that came a friendly against Austria, where Defoe would feature for an hour after replacing Michael Owen, whose thigh injury would force him out of the Croatia game. However, it was Peter Crouch who scored the only goal of the game with a header that had Defoe doing his best to get out of the way to avoid an offside flag.

But instead of pairing Crouch and Defoe for the winner-take-all match against Croatia at Wembley, McLaren opted for a cautious 4-5-1 formation with Crouch playing as the lone striker. It was to prove a catastrophic move as the visitors raced into a two-goal lead. Defoe was thrown on along with David Beckham – restored to the England set-up once the coach had realised how much the talismanic midfielder could offer – and both men got England back into the match. Defoe crept into the area almost unnoticed by the Croatia defence and was fouled by Josip Simunic. Frank Lampard put away the penalty before Beckham crossed for Crouch to level. But England's night would end in the damp squib that the teeming rain promised as Croatia nicked the decisive goal late on. England were out, and so was McLaren. Defoe would again be denied the chance to perform in a major international tournament.

The season was in danger of going stale for Defoe. He was not playing regular first team football and his international career had stalled. His difficult spell was only made worse when he missed a last-minute penalty that would have clinched all three points for Spurs at, of all places, West Ham. As the year drew to a close the speculation over his future increased, with Portsmouth emerging as clear favourites for his signature. Ironically, the months leading up to the transfer window would see Defoe enter his best goalscoring run of the season.

In early December he came face-to-face with Sven-Göran Eriksson for the first time since being dropped from England's World Cup party. The Swede was now managing Manchester City and Defoe gave the former England coach a reminder of who he should have picked to take to Germany in 2006, coming off the bench to net a late winner. 'It's a little bit late if he wants to prove a point to me today,' said Eriksson to the press after the game. 'I will not be the next man for the job.' But even with Keane suspended, new manager Ramos refused to guarantee Defoe a place. 'It's true that Defoe definitely helps the team when he comes on,' he said, 'but I have four centre forwards I have to choose between. He's one of them.'

Defoe would score against City again in a League Cup quarter-final tie before grabbing goals in three consecutive games against Fulham, Reading and Aston Villa. But these would prove to be his last in a Tottenham shirt – for a while. He would only start two more games for Spurs, and only play a total of 35 minutes of their famous 6-1 aggregate win over Arsenal in the League Cup semi-final – the perfect revenge for last season's defeat at the same stage. The fact that Defoe was willing to miss a potential cup final appearance seemed to prove he was ready to leave White Hart Lane.

Chapter 8

Happy With Harry

Harry Redknapp had given Defoe his first chance as a professional by bringing him to West Ham as a teenager. He had also overseen the move to Bournemouth on loan that had proved to be an outstanding success. Even after leaving West Ham, Redknapp was open in his praise of Defoe's abilities and had made clear on more than one occasion that he would be interested in bringing the England striker back to the south coast as a Portsmouth player. On the last day of the January transfer window Redknapp did just that, signing Defoe for a fee of around £6 million.

The move spoke volumes about how Defoe was feeling at the time. He had not been frozen out at Spurs. He was still very much part of their plans. Added to that, the team had a League Cup final against Chelsea at Wembley to look forward to. But Defoe did not want to be a bit-part player, regardless of the circumstances. Portsmouth may not have been as glamorous a proposition as Tottenham, but the bottom line was that at Fratton Park, Defoe would be a regular in the first team. He was one of a number of players in a squad rotation system under Juande Ramos, but he would have no such worries at Pompey. His aim was to play games and score goals, and under Redknapp at Portsmouth, he would be able to do that.

It was another big-money transfer for Defoe, who had joined Spurs for a similar fee four years earlier. But the move was not all plain sailing. The clubs' struggle to agree a fee, coupled with the proximity to deadline day, meant that Defoe's initial signature for Portsmouth was on loan. He would only make one appearance as a loan player before being fully registered, but it was enough to ensure he would be ineligible for his first match after the move which, by one of those footballing twists of fate, happened to be against Spurs. It caused some frustration for player and manager, but that would not last long as Defoe got his Portsmouth career off to a flying start.

As he had scored on his debut for every team he'd played for at senior level, there was no shortage of expectation as Defoe took to the field for his Portsmouth bow against Chelsea. Just ten minutes after the Blues had taken the lead, he raced on to reach a flick from his strike partner Milan Baros and slid the ball past keeper Petr Cech into the back of the net. He had scored on his debut once more and the Pompey fans were overjoyed with their new idol. He could have gone on to win the game but was denied both by Cech and his own unsteady finishing, no doubt the result of a lack of match sharpness. That was certainly what Redknapp thought as he told the press: 'Maybe if he had been sharp he would have stuck in the winner. That'll come when he gets games under his belt.'

It was clear then that Redknapp was ready to give Defoe plenty of action as his main striker. In a squad that contained Czech international Baros, David Nugent and an ageing Kanu as its attackers, Defoe was the only player of that group who offered such a direct approach. It made him almost undroppable from the manager's point of view, which was perfect for a player who knew that regular football would give him the chance to impress the new England head coach, Fabio Capello.

After taking over from the much-derided Steve McLaren, the legendary Italian manager had set about making sure his England team would gain back the respect it had lost in failing so embarrassingly to qualify for the European Championships. Every player who was hoping to play for England was desperate to show the new boss that they were good enough to represent the country and to help to pull the team back out of the hole. Defoe was no different and having made the perfect start to 2008, he was included in Capello's first squad for a friendly against Switzerland at Wembley. Frustratingly, he was left on the bench for the entire game as England gave the new manager a 2-1 winning start.

But that would not dampen Defoe's spirits, as his new surroundings at Portsmouth helped him go from strength to strength. Another impressive performance helped the team to a 1-0 win at Bolton's Reebok Stadium, and he was again in scoring mood when Sunderland were the visitors to Fratton Park. The game would also provide the chance for Defoe to exorcise a personal demon when Pompey midfielder Niko Kranjcar went down in the penalty area. Defoe had already missed from the spot earlier in the season for Spurs against West Ham, but he was determined not to let that affect him.

'When you've missed one, you don't think about it,' he said after the game. 'It's a different occasion with a new club. It's all different, isn't it? I was confident stepping up. I've been practising penalties in training. Before the Chelsea game recently, we were in the dressing room and the gaffer asked who fancied the penalties. I didn't say anything but I think he knew. As we got the penalty, the lads looked at me and that was it. I knew what I had to do. It was just a case of trying to relax. I said to myself that I was just going to pick my spot and hit it hard.' And that was exactly what he did. Goalkeeper Craig Gordon was left with no chance as Portsmouth claimed a 1-0 win.

That same weekend in late February, Defoe's former club went to Wembley and won the League Cup final against Chelsea. To many onlookers it looked like Defoe had made the worst choice of his career. Why leave when Spurs were heading into a major cup final? Why leave when he would have a chance to feature in a showpiece event and pick up a winners' medal? The answer was simple. By leaving Spurs when he did, he had ensured he would not suffer from a prolonged spell at the lower end of the pecking order. It was all very well being part of a squad that won a trophy, but Defoe wanted more than that. He wanted to play and to score goals, and he wanted success to come as a result of it, not as an alternative to it.

As if to prove the point, he continued in rich vein of form as Portsmouth travelled to Everton. It was not to be a good day for the visitors, but in front of a watching Mr Capello, Defoe gave an early indication to the England coach that he was well worth keeping an eye on. He was used to impressing new managers at the earliest opportunity and he gave a performance the Italian could not ignore. First he darted across the area to divert home a cross from fellow England hopeful Glen Johnson to level the score at 1-1. He could then have scored again were it not for a fine block by defender Phil Jagielka. Instead two more Everton goals settled the game, but he had done more than enough to give Capello food for thought.

By now Defoe's confidence was sky high again and it was rubbing off on his new team-mates. With Defoe cup-tied, Portsmouth pulled off an astonishing shock in the quarter-finals of the FA Cup against Manchester United at Old Trafford, where Sulley Muntari's penalty was enough to take Pompey to Wembley for the semi finals. What a shame it was for Defoe, who had already missed out on one trip to the national stadium and would now be forced to miss another. However, instead of getting down in the dumps about it, he responded in the perfect way. He returned to the team for a home game against Birmingham bursting with pride at what his new colleagues had achieved. If he could not help them in their cup endeavours, he would give everything to help them in the Premier League – as Birmingham found to their cost.

First he fired Pompey ahead from the penalty spot with only six minutes gone. Just three minutes later he made it two with the simplest of tap-ins. While Birmingham managed to level the scores, they could not match Portsmouth in the second half as two more goals sealed a fine win. And with five minutes to go Defoe was made to feel even more at home as he received a rapturous ovation when Redknapp decided to substitute him late in the game. He had shot to hero status in double-quick time.

Defoe was proving a real inspiration to Portsmouth,

whether he played or not. His manager revealed to the media after the game that the striker was happier than anyone to see Portsmouth performing miracles in the cup. Redknapp said: 'The first text I got on Saturday after knocking Manchester United out of the FA Cup was from him with a message saying well done to the lads. That is what team spirit is all about. You need players like that around you.' And the boss was adamant that Defoe would be kept around for the duration, adding: 'He has missed out on two Wembley appearances this year, one with Spurs and now one with us. But we will definitely take him with us for the day.' It was a heart-warming boost for the striker, who only months before had been in danger of being left on the fringes at Spurs.

The manager would be heaping more praise on Defoe as his sixth goal in as many appearances in a Portsmouth shirt brought another win, this time at home to Aston Villa thanks to a deft finish over the goalkeeper. It was a feat made all the more impressive by the fact that the striker had just fought off a stomach bug to take his place on the pitch. 'He's got that knack, that goalscorer's instinct,' Redknapp told journalists. 'He's had it since he was 15 when I first signed him.' But one man who was not yet fully convinced was Fabio Capello, who could not find a place for him in England's friendly against France in Paris, a match England lost. But far worse was to come for Defoe.

Just days before Portsmouth's next game at home to Wigan, Defoe's grandmother passed away. It was a tragic moment in the life of a young man whose family was so important to him, but his response was a positive one. After scoring the first of two goals he removed his shirt to reveal a t-shirt bearing the message 'RIP, Nan – I love you'. The letter of the law meant he had to be booked but manager Redknapp, himself a dedicated family man, had no trouble forgiving his grieving star. It was another display of mental strength from Defoe, who would be out of the team for the upcoming FA Cup semi-final against West Brom. One would never have guessed anything was wrong – his two goals set a Portsmouth record as his total raced to eight goals in seven matches.

Those two were his final goals of the season as the 2007/08 campaign came to a bittersweet end. His record-breaking run had helped Portsmouth to their highest ever Premier League finish of eighth, but he had missed more than his fair share of days out at Wembley. Not only did he miss the semi-final against West Brom, but Pompey's victory meant Defoe would have to sit out the final against Cardiff, from which they emerged brandishing the FA Cup. Defoe had played for two clubs during the season and both had won a major domestic trophy. Yet he had no medals to show for their success.

That, though, would not hinder his progress. His form since moving to Portsmouth had only improved, so it was no surprise when Capello called up Defoe to the England squad for their summer fixtures. In an ideal world, Defoe would have been lining up with the national team for the European Championships, rather than a pair of friendly internationals against the USA at home and Trinidad & Tobago away. However, for Defoe it did not matter what the context of the games was. All that mattered was that he would be given the chance to start up front in both games.

He was determined to make an impact in both fixtures and that is exactly what he did. Having missed out on the Wembley finals, he was not about to let this chance to showcase himself at the home of English football pass him by.

Against the Americans he was quick to get himself into the game and, alongside Wayne Rooney, he was a continual threat to the US defenders. He very nearly set up his strike partner with chances in the first half, before going close himself after getting ahead of his marker in the penalty area but firing wide. In the second half he had another shot well saved and was involved in the decisive goal, finding Gareth Barry who set up Steven Gerrard to seal a 2-0 victory.

Despite not getting a goal and being substituted in the second half, Defoe had done enough to earn a starting place for the trip to the Caribbean. A warm early summer's evening had the atmosphere of a holiday rather than an international football fixture. Things were not helped by the somewhat cynical view of some onlookers, who saw the fixture as nothing more than an exercise to help England's bid to host the 2018 World Cup by securing the vote of FIFA Executive Committee member and (regional football federation) CONCACAF president Jack Warner.

However, that was of no concern to Defoe, who soon made sure that people would leave the Hasely Crawford Stadium talking about what happened on the pitch, not off it. This time he was playing alongside West Ham striker Dean Ashton, who was making his international debut, but Defoe was to be the dominant performer. After Barry had given the visitors an early lead, Defoe took the game by the scruff of the neck with two goals of his own. First he ended a storming run down the left channel with a fine finish one-on-one with the goalkeeper after a quarter of an hour, then he netted with a close-range strike in the second half, after substitute David Bentley had crossed to the unmarked forward.

His fourth and fifth international goals had provided Defoe

with the international boost he had been looking for under the new head coach. He said after the game that his confidence had soared after the move to Portsmouth. 'I finished the season strongly,' he enthused. 'When a new manager comes in, everyone is on the same level. I am delighted to have got two goals. To play for your country and score is the best feeling in the world.' With a World Cup qualifying campaign set to start in the autumn, it was a feeling that Defoe was desperate to keep experiencing.

With no international tournament to keep him occupied before the start of the new season, Defoe returned to Portsmouth for the new season refreshed and ready to pick up where he'd left off. His goalscoring form at the end of the previous season had guaranteed him a place as Harry Redknapp's main goal threat. For the first time in his Premier League career, he would be the first striker on the team sheet every time. He would also have a new striker partner, but it was somebody that Defoe knew pretty well already.

Czech Republic international Milan Baros had returned to France following his loan spell from Lyon, which left room for a new centre-forward to come in alongside Defoe. Previous seasons had shown the little striker worked best with a big man alongside him, so Redknapp bought the biggest he could find. Peter Crouch now rejoined the club he had spent a season with in the early stages of his career, re-forming a strike duo that had performed well together at under-21 international level.

It was a strike force that had the potential to excite the Pompey fans and Defoe himself. 'We know how each other plays,' he told the media before the season started. 'Now it's just a case of getting fitter and sharper, and that is going to come. Overall our record is a good one. We talk to each other off the pitch and that helps us a lot. We're going to have a good season.'

The season did not get off to the greatest of starts, however. Portsmouth's FA Cup win had earned them a Community Shield date with Premier League champions Manchester United, so Defoe was back at Wembley for the annual curtain-raiser. The new partnership would not click into gear immediately, but neither would United's strike force as a disappointing 0-0 draw led to a penalty shootout. Defoe scored his spot-kick but no other Portsmouth player would be successful, while Manchester United displayed the calmness of a team that had won the Champions League on penalties the previous spring.

But the disappointing result at Wembley would do little to dampen Defoe's spirits. He had already scored against Manchester United in pre-season, having netted in a pre-season tour of Africa friendly the month before. It was one of two goals he scored on tour, the other coming against Cape Town Ajax. There were also pre-season strikes against Oxford United, Swindon, Exeter and his old club Bournemouth, so regardless of what had happened at Wembley, Defoe was already in good scoring form.

'Even in pre-season, it's always important to be scoring goals as a striker,' he said ahead of Portsmouth's opening league fixture against Chelsea. 'It helps to build confidence and I will be looking to take that into the season.' When journalists asked him about his hopes for his country, he replied: 'For all the players, England is at the back of your mind, but first and foremost we've got to get off to a good start at club level. That's what counts. If you're playing well and looking sharp, that's how you get in the squad. I fancy my chances, but you've got to forget about what you did last season. It's a new season and a fresh start for everyone – I just want to get off to a good start and hopefully the goals will come.'

The goals would come for Defoe, but not on the opening day of the season. For all the team's confidence, a trip to Stamford Bridge against a Chelsea side desperate to impress their new manager Luiz Felipe Scolari – a World-Cup-winning Brazil coach and former Portugal boss – was not going to be an easy task. The hosts cruised to an emphatic 4-0 victory, and Defoe's best chance did not come until the 78th minute when he combined with Crouch to fashion an opportunity that flew wide of Petr Cech's goal.

Defoe's battle with Cech would resume a few days later when he was picked to start up front for England in a home friendly against the Czech Republic. But again the Chelsea stopper would come out on top as he continually thwarted Defoe, who had several opportunities to increase his haul of international goals. The striker was substituted at half-time, although – despite his failing to find the net – it appeared a harsh decision as his pace on the attack remained a threat. It seemed inevitable that one of the Czech goalscorers in the 2-2 draw would be the man who had preceded Defoe at Portsmouth – Milan Baros.

Things would not get any easier for Portsmouth. Having started the season away at Chelsea, their next task was to take on Manchester United at Fratton Park. Pompey huffed and puffed but could not break United down. Nor could Defoe beat the offside trap, as his attempts to play on the shoulder of the last defender were regularly punished by the linesman's flag. A deflected goal from Scotland midfielder Darren Fletcher sealed Portsmouth's fate, but Harry Redknapp remained upbeat. 'When we settle down and understand each other a bit more we'll be OK,' he said. How right he was.

Away fixtures at Everton are never easy, but having played two of the Premier League's big guns in quick succession, Portsmouth feared no one. Despite not having opened his account for the season, Defoe was confident he could break his duck soon enough and he did not have much longer to wait. Not only that, his fledgling partnership with Crouch was to pay dividends as well, as the pair combined to devastating effect for the first time.

With 12 minutes on the clock, Crouch's aerial prowess caused havoc in the Everton back line. His flick found Defoe who, despite being surrounded by five Everton defenders, powered in a clinical finish to open the scoring in style. Just before half-time Defoe would turn creator with a neat pass to Glen Johnson, who put away Portsmouth's second. A penalty save from David James ensured the visitors kept a clean sheet before Crouch and Defoe wrapped up the win in style, Defoe's delightful chip from 20 yards bouncing down off the bar and appearing to cross the line before Crouch made sure it did.

It was a fantastic performance from Defoe, and with a pair of World Cup qualifiers on the way it was a huge statement to Fabio Capello, who was becoming increasingly impressed with the 25-year-old. After the game Defoe said of the England boss: 'When you see that a manager has faith in you and he plays you, you feel great. To be honest, it hasn't been like this before. Maybe with the new manager this is the first time I have had a decent chance with England.' It was perhaps a sly dig at Sven-Göran Eriksson, but more likely an indication of genuine excitement that the new national coach would give a chance to any player, providing he was fit and on form.

Another chance is what Defoe got with another crack at Andorra, against whom he had scored two years earlier. But England's performance away from home was far from convincing and Capello hauled Defoe off the pitch at half-time with the score goalless against one of European football's smallest minnows. Defoe's former West Ham companion Joe Cole would spare England's blushes with two second-half goals but the damage was done for Defoe, who would be left out of the next game in Croatia altogether. England won that game 4-1, exacting revenge for their Euro 2008 heartache, with a hat-trick for Theo Walcott of all people. The man who had taken Defoe's place for the last World Cup had inadvertently forced him into the background again.

And the background was no place for Defoe. While he was far more delighted with England's win than disappointed at missing out, he still wanted to keep himself in the national squad. The way to do that was to score more goals, so a brace at home to Middlesbrough was the perfect response to the blank against Andorra. Boro had taken the lead through Defoe's old partner Mido, but the latest little-and-large double act would have the last word. A knockdown from Crouch set Defoe free to smash the ball into the net. The win was confirmed four minutes from time when Defoe slammed home with the kind of poacher's goal he rarely missed.

This time, it was Crouch's turn to lavish praise on his partner. 'Jermain's got a good touch outside the box, but inside it I don't think I've played with anyone better who's such a natural finisher,' he enthused. 'Give him a chance and invariably he'll put it away. That's a great armoury to have and if I can play to his strengths and get my fair share of goals we'll do well this year. I've seen a lot of fantastic players and fantastic finishers. There are people who run him close but around the box people will agree he's a fantastic finisher and given chances he'll score a bundle of goals.'

He was given more chances as Portsmouth embarked on the first European tie in their 110-year history. Victory in the FA Cup had catapulted Pompey into the UEFA Cup and the historic night was made all the more special with a victory over Portuguese club Guimaraes. After France midfielder Lassana Diarra had exchanged passes with Defoe before thumping in a net-bulging volley, Defoe himself had the chance to make it two from the penalty spot. Unfortunately, goalkeeper Correa Junior Nilson would deny him but Defoe made amends with a volley of his own to cement the victory. After the game, Guimaraes coach Manuel Cajuda admitted his side had worried too much about the height of Peter Crouch. 'We were concerned about their big player,' he said, 'but it was the two smallest players who scored.'

Unfortunately the next couple of games would not go Defoe's – or Portsmouth's – way. He barely got a sniff at goal at Manchester City as Pompey crashed to a humiliating 6-0 defeat – a result that was out of character after three wins in a row. Things went from bad to worse as they crashed to a 4-0 loss against Chelsea in the League Cup at Fratton Park, although Defoe remained on the bench for the duration of that dismal encounter.

Defoe returned to the side for the next Premier League game, at home against his former club Tottenham. Things at White Hart Lane had changed dramatically since he had departed. Under Juande Ramos Spurs had begun the season in a dreadful fashion. They were rooted to the foot of the table and could not buy a win at home or away. Defoe would show them no remorse as he ignored cries of 'You're Spurs and you know you are' from the Tottenham faithful to drive home a first-half penalty. He then had a hand in Crouch's winner, setting up on-loan Arsenal defender Armand Traore whose shot was parried into the striker's path by Spurs keeper Heurelho Gomes. Refreshingly, Defoe was applauded off the pitch by both sets of fans when he was replaced by another ex-Spurs man, Younes Kaboul, with a minute to go.

With four goals in his last four games Defoe was again on a goalscoring run. Despite failing to get on the scoresheet in more than 100 minutes of the second leg against Guimaraes as Portsmouth made hard work of progressing to the UEFA Cup group stage, he showed no signs of tiredness and was again among the scorers when Pompey played host to Premier League new boys Stoke. The Potters struggled to cope as the Defoe-Crouch connection saw them off with great aplomb. Defoe's pass to Crouch was finished off with a spectacular bicycle kick from the big man, and although Stoke cancelled that goal out, Defoe was on hand to drive home a right-footed shot to guarantee all three points. Between them, Crouch and Defoe had scored 11 goals already – and the season had only just reached October.

With five goals in his past five matches, Defoe had to be in contention for a starting place for England's first home World Cup qualifier against lowly Kazakhstan. However, again he would have to make do with a place on the bench as Capello favoured the physical presence of Emile Heskey and the raw pace of Theo Walcott alongside Wayne Rooney up front.

However, with England 4-1 to the good, Defoe was given a brief run-out and reminded the head coach that he was very much a man in form with the fifth goal. His 26th birthday had come the previous week, but the 27th year of his life was to begin with a major shake-up.

As October progressed, all was about to change at Portsmouth. In the same week as they were beaten in their opening UEFA Cup group game by Braga of Portugal, Tottenham Hotspur were beaten in their corresponding fixture by Italian club Udinese. That defeat was the final straw for the Spurs board, who sacked Juande Ramos with immediate effect. Just days later Harry Redknapp left Portsmouth to take the vacant position at White Hart Lane. Having managed West Ham, Portsmouth and Southampton in the Premier League, he felt a move to north London would give him the opportunity to manage one of the biggest clubs in the country – despite the fact that they were bottom of the table with just two points from their first eight games of the season.

This left Defoe at something of a career crossroads. Redknapp had played a prominent role in his footballing education since his teenage years and kept a keen eye on his progress before bringing him to Portsmouth. What was he to do now? Should he continue to focus his attention on the club that paid his wages, or try to engineer a move away to rejoin his former manager in January? Defoe was not the only player with such concerns. Individuals such as Peter Crouch and Lassana Diarra had joined the club on the back of the impression the manager had made on them. As furious as Portsmouth's fans were at Redknapp's decision, they were equally worried that their best players would follow him out of the door.

Those fears were not helped when new manager Tony Adams made it clear that any player who wanted to leave the club in January would be allowed to do so. It was an understandable stance for the former Arsenal defender and Pompey assistant manager to take in his first Premier League management job. He knew that if Portsmouth were to recover from their recent upheaval, he would need every single player pulling in the same direction. He told the media on his takeover: 'I want players who want to play for Portsmouth. If I was the manager at Arsenal one day and somebody came to me and said, "I do not want to play for Arsenal," I would still say I would let them go. That is 100 per cent, that is crystal clear, because if they do not want to play for Portsmouth it does no good in the long run. We have some very good players at this football club and it is my job to keep them here.'

The new manager's presence seemed to have a positive effect. Portsmouth were unlucky not to win in a 1-1 draw with Fulham, in which Defoe was involved in the opening goal, setting up Crouch to keep the potency of their strike partnership at a high level. An encouraging performance in a 1-0 defeat at Liverpool followed but the new manager decided to keep Defoe on the bench until the late stages, preferring to play with one striker in an away fixture against top-quality opposition. A disappointing home defeat to Wigan followed, but Portsmouth were still looking comfortable in the top half of the table.

A visit to the Stadium of Light would bring Adams his first win as Portsmouth manager thanks to Defoe's late, late winner. Pompey had gone a goal behind early on but the players showed great resolve to get themselves back in the game, and when El Hadji Diouf fouled Glen Johnson in the penalty area in the last minute, Defoe needed to be courageous in the face of ribbing from defender Anton Ferdinand. 'He was giving me a bit of stick to try to put me off,' said Defoe. 'He came up to me and was saying: "You're not going to score, you're not going to score." I said: "Trust me, I'm going to score."' He did.

He also did his best after the game to quieten the voices suggesting that he would be one of the first players to follow Harry Redknapp to White Hart Lane. 'I've had speculation since I was a kid,' he said. 'It's part and parcel of being a footballer. You don't think about speculation. Obviously Harry brought me to Portsmouth and I was with him at West Ham.'

Despite not denying he would rejoin Tottenham at some point, he added words of support for his new manager: 'I'm a Portsmouth player and I will continue working hard. I'm enjoying my time here. I'm scoring goals and I am part of a good team. We are pushing up the table so why would I think about leaving? And anyway, Tony is trying to build something here. He's a good manager and training has been fantastic all week. I am playing with good players and for me that is the most important thing.'

However, he would not be as happy in Portsmouth's following game, as he failed with three excellent opportunities against West Ham at Upton Park, thwarted on all three occasions by Hammers keeper Robert Green. But those missed chances evidently did not worry Fabio Capello, who selected Defoe to start in England's friendly against Germany at Munich's Olympiastadion. It was a depleted England team that took to the field but goals in each half from centre-backs Matthew Upson and John Terry sealed an impressive 2-1 win for the visitors. More pressingly for Defoe, he was forced off at half-time with a calf injury that threatened to keep him out for a number of weeks. Fortunately the diagnosis was not as serious as first thought.

The disappointment for Defoe was that the injury would keep him out of one of the most famous nights in Portsmouth's history as they played host to Italian giants AC Milan in the UEFA Cup. His team-mates were magnificent as they raced into a 2-0 lead, only to be pegged back late in the game to draw 2-2. Perhaps with Defoe's extra firepower they might have won the game, but that could take nothing away from the Pompey players who performed so heroically in a fixture regarded by many fans as a once-in-a-lifetime event.

Defoe would return at the end of November for a home game against Blackburn Rovers, when he also found himself back among the goals as Tony Adams claimed his first win at Fratton Park. The Crouch-Defoe forward line put Blackburn on the back foot, with Crouch's headed opener being followed up by Defoe speeding through to double Portsmouth's lead. Two goals in five minutes brought the Lancashire side level, but Sean Davis grabbed a late winner to ensure Pompey finished the month in eighth place.

Defoe's goalscoring form continued into December with the equalising goal in Portsmouth's next UEFA Cup engagement, against Wolfsburg in Germany. However, it was a bad night for the visitors as they crashed to a 3-2 defeat, which ultimately ended their maiden season in European football. It had been an enjoyable adventure for Pompey, but it was to be their final game in European football for the time being. It was also to be Jermain Defoe's final goal in Pompey blue.

After Michael Owen had scored one of three Newcastle goals in a 3-0 victory over Portsmouth at St James' Park,

Adams insisted he would rather have Defoe in his side than the experienced England striker. However, his praise would fall on deaf ears as the days counted down to the January transfer window. Failure to score in the next two games left Defoe increasingly frustrated with life on the south coast and it was becoming impossible to look at the sports pages of a newspaper without seeing a story linking the 26-year-old with a move back to Tottenham Hotspur.

Adams left Defoe out for Portsmouth's 1-0 defeat against his old club Arsenal, and admitted the England player was not happy after missing the game. 'Jermain was really annoyed with me for leaving me out and he is still angry with me now,' Adams said in his post-match press conference. 'He's a fantastic player, scores great goals but at the moment we are struggling with balance. Away at Liverpool and away at Arsenal I chose to keep him on the bench. Those are my reasons and speculate all you want but I have had no offers for Jermain Defoe, not one.' That would not be the case for much longer.

The New Year brought the opening of the transfer window and within days the national media had confirmed Defoe was seeking a move away from Fratton Park and a return to working with Redknapp. Portsmouth's executive chairman Peter Storrie confirmed to the *Portsmouth News* that Defoe wanted to go back to Tottenham, but the price initially seemed too high. Redknapp claimed his former club were seeking in excess of £20 million for the striker – a price that he was not willing to pay, even for a striker he knew could do a job for him. Defoe just wanted to leave as quickly as possible.

'I've enjoyed my time immensely here,' he told the press, 'but I can't deny that Harry Redknapp's departure as manager hit me hard, particularly because he was the primary reason why I joined Portsmouth in the first place and said so at the time.'

He did insist, though, that Tony Adams's appointment as manager had nothing to do with his decision. 'I have a great deal of respect for Tony Adams and what he's trying to achieve,' he added. 'We have a very good working relationship. But I left Tottenham to join Portsmouth with the intention of working with Harry for a considerable time to come. So it was obviously a big blow when he left and particularly when he went back to my former club. I could have gone to other clubs when I left Tottenham but I wanted to work with Harry. I always said that if I got regular first team football I'd repay him with goals and I've delivered on that promise. And I enjoy being around him because he brings out the best of me and that is all you can ask for from a manager.'

It seemed that 'come and get me' plea was enough for the clubs to agree (after long negotiations) a fee of around £15 million to take Defoe back to White Hart Lane. Despite claiming he had received death threats from Portsmouth fans, Defoe re-signed for the north London club and was unveiled at White Hart Lane before Tottenham's 4-1 League Cup semi-final first leg win over Burnley. Even though he had been a hero at Portsmouth, and despite the good times he acknowledged having there, the actions of some of their fans left a bitter taste in Defoe's mouth. The Tottenham faithful, however, were delighted to see him back.

The start of 2009 was certainly eventful for Defoe. Within the space of ten days he had become a Tottenham player again – less than six months after expressing his excitement about the season to come with Portsmouth. It was a prime example of how quickly things can change in football. But for Defoe there was no time to look back. Just two days after signing a new five-year contract with Spurs, he was lining up for his second debut for the club in an away fixture at Wigan Athletic. Unfortunately he would not continue his remarkable record of scoring on his debut – even worse, the visitors came away having lost 1-0. But Defoe did not have too long a wait on his hands to re-open his Tottenham Hotspur scoring account.

His first game back at White Hart Lane could only be against one team. Portsmouth's travelling fans were vociferous in their treatment of Messrs Redknapp and Defoe, but it was to little avail as their star of 2008 scored an equaliser with 20 minutes left to prevent the ultimate revenge for Pompey. However, the game would be remembered for the contribution of another Tottenham striker – and the man whose arrival reportedly hastened Defoe's initial departure from the Lane – Darren Bent. After somehow missing a completely free header from inside the six-yard box and right in front of goal, Redknapp uttered the now immortal phrase: 'I think my missus could have scored that.'

The goal that Defoe scored was a fine one, and only served to remind Portsmouth of the quality of the player who had left them. The striker started and finished the move by releasing the ball and following some neat interplay between Didier Zokora and Luka Modric, receiving it back and zipping a shot through Sol Campbell and beyond David James. He even had a chance to win the game for Tottenham late on, but for now an equalising goal against his former club would suffice.

Defoe's move back to Spurs also presented him another crack at getting to a Wembley final. Despite not being registered at Tottenham in time to take part in the first leg of their League

Cup semi-final against Burnley, he had not featured for Portsmouth in the competition and so would not be cup-tied for the return leg at Turf Moor. With the Londoners in such a commanding position going into the game, it was unthinkable that they would not reach the final for the second season in succession. However, despite their big lead, Burnley would prove no pushovers, having already knocked out Premier League heavyweights Arsenal and Chelsea.

Not only were Burnley no pushovers, they were simply phenomenal. Goals from Robbie Blake, Chris McCann and substitute Jay Rodriguez sealed a 3-0 win on the night, levelling the aggregate score at 4-4 and forcing the tie into extra time. The Clarets also held the advantage of having scored an away goal, which would come into play should the tie finish level. However, with just two minutes left, Tottenham's Russian striker Roman Pavlyuchenko emerged from the bench to slot home and break Burnley's hearts. Defoe added the gloss with a sweetly struck curling shot in the final moments. Spurs were going back to Wembley and finally Defoe could look forward to playing a final there.

But before he could think about that, Tottenham had the FA Cup to contend with. A 1-0 defeat by Manchester United put paid to their hopes of a domestic cup double, as Defoe's 19-minute cameo from the bench could not turn the tide in his team's favour. However, there were plenty of points to play for in the Premier League, starting with a home game against Stoke City at the end of January. The Staffordshire side had impressed in their most recent spell in the top division, but they would come unstuck at White Hart Lane as Defoe scored his third goal in four starts since rejoining Spurs.

After Aaron Lennon had scored the opener, Defoe was

released behind the visiting defence and drove home with a clinical finish. Michael Dawson headed in a third before half-time and the game was over, despite a consolation goal in the second half from James Beattie. It was an important win for Tottenham as they still had plenty to do pull themselves away from the wrong end of the table. While they maintained their ambitions were to earn a place in Europe by the end of the season – still very much a possibility – they first had to ensure that they would not be sucked back into a relegation battle.

Sadly, Defoe would play very little part in helping to achieve this. Shortly after the Stoke victory he fractured a metatarsal bone in his foot in a freak training-ground injury. It was the sort of injury that had hindered such England stars as David Beckham and Wayne Rooney in the past, and now it had hit Defoe. While there would be no World Cup place at risk in the summer that followed, the injury did rule him out of the League Cup final against Manchester United. It was desperately unlucky for Defoe – he had now missed out on three Wembley finals in two seasons through no fault of his own. Spurs would lose the final on penalties, and by the time Defoe returned in his team's 1-0 win over Newcastle in April, the race for Europe was very much on. But that would soon be the last thing on Defoe's mind.

Just a few days after the Newcastle game, news emerged that Defoe's half-brother Jade had been killed in a street attack in Leytonstone, east London. It was an appallingly tragic event, not least for the unnecessary death of a 26-year-old musician, but also for Defoe and his close-knit family. It was testament to Defoe's strength of character and the love and support of his family behind him that he would be able to play until the end of the season with such a horrible event at the front of his mind.

One more goal was all Defoe had to show for the end of the campaign, and it came in the penultimate match of the campaign at home to Manchester City. However, there was at least one lighter moment during the game that brought the gleaming smile back to his face. His opening goal was preceded by another effort that was disallowed for offside, before Defoe was involved in a bizarre collision with linesman Trevor Massey, which resulted in the official having to leave the field injured. He had been out for some three months but Defoe could not be kept out of the spotlight on the pitch! Robbie Keane scored the winning goal for Spurs but a final-day defeat at Liverpool meant that the club finished eighth and missed out on Europe by two points.

On the pitch it had been another eventful season for Defoe in both club and international football. His new club had recovered from their abysmal start to finish the season strongly, and in rejoining Tottenham under Harry Redknapp it seemed as though he had finally found his true home in the Premier League. Despite his late-season injury, he had cemented his place in Fabio Capello's immediate plans for England as qualification for the World Cup in South Africa began to hot up. Next season would be an important one on that front, with Defoe determined to avoid the situation he had been in four years ago. He knew if he could start the new season well, he would give himself every chance to play in the first major international tournament of his career.

But off the pitch, there was a void. He and Jade had been great friends as well as half-brothers. Family had always been so important to Defoe and with the loss of his grandmother being followed so quickly by another tragedy, it would take all of his determination and inner strength to recover psychologically. However, when he was finally ready at the start of the following season to talk about what had happened, it was clear that both his mind and his heart were firmly in the right place.

Chapter 9

Triumph After Tragedy

The summer of 2009 and the subsequent 2009/10 season were to be of great significance to Jermain Defoe in footballing terms. He had World Cup qualification with England to consider as well as a new campaign with Tottenham as they looked to force their way into the top four of the Premier League and a place in the Champions League. But however important his football was, it was nothing compared to the importance of his family after the loss of his half-brother Jade.

In September 2009 Defoe revealed how his mother had arrived unexpectedly at the Spurs training ground. She was there to deliver the awful news that Jade, having been in intensive care, had just hours to live. His condition had deteriorated seriously since the attack. 'I remember I was training on the Friday before the Manchester United game and my mum turned up,' he recalled to the national press.

205

'The manager said to me, "Your mum's in the car park." I knew straight away when I saw her face. She basically just said to me, "I think he's got two hours to live." So I had to get myself to the hospital and just be there for him. I actually missed the United game but there are more important things than football. It was crazy. All the family were there and his close friends.'

While Jade and Jermain shared a father who had left his wife and son some years ago, the two young men also shared a close bond. Jade was a promising musician and rapper on the 'grime' scene in London, and while his footballer half-brother lived an entirely different life on a seemingly different planet, they were as close as any pair of brothers would be. Indeed Jermain referred to Jade as his 'brother', ditching the 'half' prefix. They enjoyed each other's company as they did the company of the whole family. It was fitting at least that the entire family would come together for Jade, albeit in the most harrowing of circumstances.

Family had always come first for Defoe. Just a year before he had lost his grandmother and been similarly shaken. 'It was strange,' he told the media. 'Look at my brother. He was 26 years old. You don't expect to see that. When people are ill it's easier to understand when they die. You prepare yourself. You know it's going to happen at some time. But when it's like it was with Jade and you just get the phone call it's really not easy.' He explained that their closeness made the loss all the more difficult to deal with, but at the same time he could take solace in the fact that he had a close-knit group of relatives who could help him – and whom he could help in return – to get through the toughest of times.

The tattoos on Defoe's arms speak volumes – he has the

names of his mother, grandmother, sister and brother all permanently etched onto his skin. His love for them is reflected in the love that they had shown, do show and will continue to show for him. The loving environment of his family, coupled with the faith Defoe had in his religion, would make this awful time possible to recover and indeed draw strength from.

And of course, he had football. It was the one thing that Defoe had always been able to fall back on, the one place where he could find an escape from the hard times and the one place where he could find, as he acknowledges himself, peace. It was within football that Defoe could draw on the experiences of fellow players who had also gone through times of family tragedy. He could draw inspiration from the way in which his former West Ham team-mate Frank Lampard gave his heart and soul in every game in the wake of his mother's passing in 2008. He in turn could offer sympathy to his Tottenham colleague Wilson Palacios after the Honduras international learned of the kidnap and brutal murder of his 16-year-old brother in his home country.

Perhaps it seems trivial but the way Defoe came across in the aftermath of this terrible experience was impressive. Here was a young man in tune with his emotions and aware of what was truly important in life. Values of love, family and friendship had evidently been deeply instilled in him by his mother and grandmother as he grew up. They were part of the man's very being, despite being a side of him that few people chose to see because of the public perception that had shadowed him.

Professional footballers in England have never had the best reputation. They have been known as drinkers, revellers and womanisers even before the days of Manchester United and Northern Ireland legend George Best – probably the finest British footballer of all time. That reputation has followed many of the country's finest players for generations and, whether justified or not, will continue to follow them. Footballers are now seen as regularly on the front pages of newspapers as they are on the back pages. One only has to think about the scandal involving former England captain John Terry's widely reported extra-marital affair with the ex-girlfriend of his old friend at Chelsea, Wayne Bridge, to realise just how prominent football players have become in the British public eye.

Sometimes for these gifted young professionals the trappings of fame and fortune can be too tempting, and perhaps in the early stages of his career Defoe too fell victim to temptation. Certainly the national tabloid press were only too happy to catalogue his private life and his relationships with a series of famous and glamorous young women. Irrespective of how well he would do on the pitch, he would be one of many players who would be closely scrutinised for his actions off it.

As a youngster at West Ham he was the subject of media attention for his relationship with Joanne Beckham, sister of David. That was only the start of years of tabloid investigation into his private and personal life. Things would come to a head in 2007 when the red-top press picked up on a relationship between Defoe and glamour model Danielle Lloyd after he had been engaged to marry Charlotte Mears, another model and friend of Lloyd. Throughout late 2007 the *Sunday Star* would keep the story in the public eye by trying to play the two women off against each other, publishing stories containing quotes from so-called sources and 'close friends' that Mears was trying to win him back and that the friendship between the two women was over. At a time when Defoe was trying to concentrate on football during a crucial period for Tottenham, he did not need to be at the centre of a love triangle that some newspapers were determined to keep bringing to the public's attention.

Further allegations would appear in the *Daily Star* in early 2008 as Defoe's subsequent relationship with Lloyd was said to have hit the rocks after further allegations in the press that he had been secretly seeing another woman. Defoe could no longer keep his silence and eventually told the newspaper, 'There are people out there just trying to hurt us.' He wanted to focus on his football but he could not do so as the newspapers kept on ensuring that the private lives of the country's footballers were anything but private.

Defoe would again be forced to defend himself in March 2008 as claims of him being a 'love rat' came to the fore. His relationship with Lloyd, who has since dated other professional footballers, had come to an end after he was again alleged to have been seeing somebody else behind her back. He was gaining a reputation that he felt he did not deserve. His frustration finally reached breaking point.

'I can't do anything any more,' he told the *Sunday Star*. 'Even if I chat to another girl people know about it. Everyone thinks I'm this big bad love rat – but I'm not. I just want to play football. I score goals and am doing things on the pitch but all people want to chat about is my personal life. My mum and aunties have to read all the stuff that's getting said about me. It's really upsetting them as I'm a good Catholic boy who goes to church and I don't drink. Yes, I like going to clubs but

I'm not rolling out of them drunk or anything. I just want everyone to leave me alone to get on with what I do best – scoring goals.'

His outburst was impassioned but somewhat justified. Perhaps his behaviour had not been ideal and perhaps there had been an element of naivety on his part for allowing the amount of press intrusion he had done, but he was a footballer who was far more deserving of recognition for his football. He had spent his whole life trying to impress onlookers with his ability on the pitch. He did not want the public to concern themselves with what he did off it. It was nobody else's business but his own.

However, that did not stop the tabloids targeting him again for the beginning and end of his relationships with former *Big Brother* reality TV contestants Chantelle Houghton and Imogen Thomas, and glamour girl Roxy Townsend. He was even linked to former model and reality television star Katie Price, aka Jordan. It seemed there was no way for Defoe to escape the glare of the tabloid flashbulbs, but there was always one person who would be right behind him. 'There's only room for one woman in my life,' Defoe told the *Mirror* in November 2009, 'and that's my mum. She's my number one. The other girls come and go. But no one can contend with her – or cook like her!'

It all came back to family in the end for Defoe. As much as the tabloids wanted to paint a picture of a young English footballer obsessed with money and women, it was clear with everything he said that he was nothing more than a young man who loved his family. Yes, he would go out and meet glamorous women and yes, he had been in his fair share of relationships with them, but home remains very much where his heart is. It was just a tragedy that it had to take the heartbreaking loss of a loved one for outsiders to realise that Defoe really was a good man.

Summer 2009 was a complicated one for Defoe to get through. His number one concern was making sure his family remained strong through one of the toughest periods they would ever have to endure. Meanwhile he also had plenty to concern himself with when it came to football. England had a crucial pair of qualifiers to play as they continued their quest for a World Cup place for the following year, and Defoe was again a part of Fabio Capello's squad for a trip to Kazakhstan and another date with little Andorra, against whom he had scored in 2006, at Wembley.

Again it was against Andorra that Defoe would shine. England were 4-0 winners against Kazakhstan but the Spurs man would not feature until the 80th minute and by then the game was well won. When Andorra came to Wembley a few days later on a warm June evening he was on the bench again, but this time he emerged at half-time with England three goals to the good. The simple aim was to ensure England came out of the game with not only the points in the bag, but with a healthy goal difference to set them up for the remainder of the qualifying campaign.

With 17 minutes of the game left his former Portsmouth colleague Glen Johnson crossed for Defoe to head home expertly. Headed goals were a rarity for one of the national team's smaller strikers and he enjoyed every moment of nodding in his seventh international goal. He did not have to wait too long for his eighth. Within three minutes a free-kick from David Beckham, winning his 112th England cap, was parried by keeper Koldo Alvarez and Defoe was there to convert the rebound with ease. Another goal from Peter Crouch ensured England were comfortable 6-0 winners and in doing so Capello's men maintained a 100 per cent record in their qualifying group.

Back at Tottenham, preparations were well under way for the big season ahead. After the disappointment of missing out on Europe the year before, Harry Redknapp knew his team had a lot of work to do to make a better fist of finishing in the top four and qualifying for the Champions League. To do so he invested in a number of key areas and made changes to the squad. With injury worries in defence he signed Sebastian Bassong from relegated Newcastle, and at the attacking end of the pitch he reunited Defoe with his favourite partner Peter Crouch, signing the beanpole striker for around £9 million – a deal financed by the sale of Darren Bent to Sunderland.

Pre-season allowed Spurs to take on strong opposition as they faced both Barcelona and Celtic in the inaugural Wembley Cup at the national stadium, and then the Premier League Asia Cup in the Far East, where they defeated Hull and West Ham. The final friendly of the summer came at the Lane against Greek champions Olympiakos, when Defoe came off the bench to net the final goal in a 3-0 win with a smart solo run and finish from the edge of the box. It was a significant moment for Defoe. The man he replaced was Robbie Keane, who had struggled for form since returning to Spurs after a disappointing spell at Liverpool. It was Keane who had kept Defoe out of the Spurs side for so long under Martin Jol, but now it looked as though the tide had turned in the Englishman's favour.

But before the Premier League season took centre stage,

there was more international action to distract England's players with a friendly against a strong Holland side in Amsterdam. Capello decided to pair Wayne Rooney and Emile Heskey up front, leaving Defoe on the bench again, despite his impressive second-half cameo against Andorra two months earlier. However, goals from Liverpool's Dirk Kuyt and Rafael van der Vaart of Real Madrid saw the visitors two goals down at half-time. A supersub was needed, and England had just the man.

Just four minutes after replacing Heskey at the break, Defoe's pace and speed of thought enabled him to race onto a long ball and hold off the challenge of defender Edson Braafheid before finishing excellently. His industry was further rewarded in the late stages of the game when fellow substitute James Milner beat his man and crossed for him to divert home his second goal and England's equaliser. The game finished at 2-2, although Defoe had the chances to seal a win for England. However, the coach was quick to praise the Spurs forward after the game. 'I think Defoe is one of the best English strikers there is,' he told the press. 'He's very fast, technically he's good and he's always in front of the goal.'

The praise was music to Defoe's ears. He was in good form and the England coach had singled him out for praise, despite being a man who rarely commented on individual performances. Not only that, it had put him right at the front of the coach's mind when international rivals Heskey and Michael Owen were struggling for form and fitness respectively. Defoe hailed the Holland game as his best for England so far, and explained to the media how keen he was to impress in an England shirt.

'What happened to me in the last World Cup is a massive

motivation for me,' he said. 'Sometimes people say disappointment is a blessing. If things go your way all the time in life then you may be complacent. You want that fire in your belly and this time I definitely have that because of what happened in 2006. I definitely don't want to go through that again.'

Apart from Capello, there was someone else who Defoe had really impressed with his double in Amsterdam – someone who had stuck with him every step of the way. 'After the game she was on the phone crying,' smiled Defoe. 'I was like, "Come on mum, please!"' If there were two things Defoe was desperate to do this season, they were to guarantee a place in Fabio Capello's World Cup plans and to make his mother proud, particularly after the year they had been through. As the 2009/10 season dawned, he would do both.

Defoe was ready for the start of the season and so were Tottenham. On the opening day they took on Liverpool, last season's runners-up, at White Hart Lane. Most experts believed this would be the start of a crucial season for the Reds, who were viewed as serious title contenders. However, the day would go to Spurs after a great strike from full-back Benoit Assou-Ekotto and a debut goal from new boy Bassong on either side of Steven Gerrard's penalty.

Spurs were off to a winning a start and it would not take long for Defoe to transfer his fine international form to the Premier League. A few weeks before the start of the season, Defoe had been wrongfully arrested for driving offences – although Defoe had previously been convicted of a number of driving offences, on this occasion it was a mistaken charge that Essex Police were forced to apologise for after an internal clerical error. Just before Spurs' visit to Hull's KC Stadium he was stopped again in his new car for no apparent reason and sent on his way. Hull City must have wished the police had held on to him for a little longer.

Nine minutes into the game he picked up a good pass from midfielder Tom Huddlestone and gave his team the lead with a smart left-foot finish. with Spurs leading 2-1 he scored his second on the stroke of half-time with a powerful drive high into the roof of the net, putting the game beyond the Humberside club. After Robbie Keane had made it four, Defoe claimed his hat-trick with the final goal of the game – one described by *The Mirror* as 'so good that it should have been preceded by a drum roll'. His right-foot half volley was struck with such venom the ball was barely seen from the moment it left his boot until it hit the top corner of the net. His treble ensured a second straight win and brought Spurs a place at the top of the table – their best start to a season for 44 years.

While Harry Redknapp hailed an excellent team performance, he was quick to heap praise on his main goal threat. 'He is on fire,' Redknapp enthused in his post-match press conference. 'We worked hard in the gym during the summer and he is stronger than I have ever seen him – and I have known the lad since he was 14. He is strong holding the ball and even better running with it at his feet. That has made him even more explosive and he was simply unplayable tonight.'

Being unplayable was a good way for Defoe to be heading into Tottenham's third game of the season – a trip to Upton Park to face West Ham. The boos, jeers and catcalls were as prevalent as ever from the home fans, who were in no mood to forgive or forget. Unfortunately for them, Defoe knew only one way to respond to that kind of treatment. After Carlton Cole had put the Hammers in front, he presented his Spurs counterpart with a gift of an equaliser, his stray back-pass putting Defoe clean through. Almost unable to believe his luck, he lashed the ball past international team-mate Robert Green. Aaron Lennon completed the turnaround for Spurs and all of a sudden it was three wins from three.

Defoe was an unused substitute for Tottenham's first foray into the season's cup competition but Spurs still trounced Doncaster Rovers 5-1 at the Keepmoat Stadium in the second round of the League Cup. He returned to action the following weekend against Birmingham at White Hart Lane and while he did not score that day, a late, late winner from Lennon ensured the club's perfect start to the season continued. Four league wins from four.

The week that followed was a big one. A friendly for the national team at home to Slovenia would serve as a warm-up for a Wembley qualifier against Croatia that, if won, would guarantee England a place at the 2010 World Cup in South Africa. Despite Defoe's phenomenal form, however, Fabio Capello again preferred Emile Heskey as Wayne Rooney's partner because of the Villa striker's imposing size and physical strength.

But again Defoe would come off from the subs' bench to show the coach what he was capable of. England led Slovenia by a goal to nil at half-time, thanks to Frank Lampard's penalty, but for the second half Heskey made way for the Spurs man. The result was a smart finish from the edge of the box by Defoe after neat link-up play with club-mate Lennon. Slovenia scored a late consolation but their coach was in no doubt who the star of the opposition was. 'Capello should think seriously before the Croatia game about picking Defoe,' said Matjaz Kek.

Capello, however, laughed off the suggestion. 'Perhaps he would be tired if he played from the first minute,' he said. 'If he plays the second half he scores goals. That's good.'

All Defoe knew was that he was happy to be a part of the set-up, although he was desperate to play against Croatia – the team that had denied him his first crack at a major championship by ending England's Euro 2008 hopes. But now he was mature enough to know that whatever Mr Capello said went.

As it transpired, Defoe remained a substitute for Croatia's crucial visit to Wembley. He had told the press after the Slovenia game that he was prepared to play the role of impact sub if it helped the team and Capello stuck with the formula he preferred. It worked perfectly. Not only did England win, they trounced the Croats 5-1 to exorcise any demons remaining from 2007. England were going to South Africa. While Defoe played only 30 minutes and did not score, he was as overjoyed as every other player on the pitch – not to mention most of the 87,000 fans packed into Wembley and millions more around the country. Capello had accomplished his first mission as England boss.

With England's summer plans confirmed, Defoe now had something else to play for. While finishing in the top four with Tottenham remained the main priority, he knew a continuation of his good form for the rest of the season would guarantee him a place among the final 23 names that Capello would take to Africa. However, the weeks that followed would prove difficult.

Reigning champions Manchester United were the first visitors to White Hart Lane following England's glorious night. Both sides boasted strikers who had serious aspirations of making it to South Africa – Defoe at Spurs and the ever-imposing Wayne Rooney for the Red Devils. While the latter would have the last laugh on the day, the former would get the game off to a scintillating start.

Defoe's old Spurs strike partner Dimitar Berbatov was playing alongside Rooney for United and it was his loose pass in the first minute that gifted possession to Tottenham. The ball eventually found its way to Assou-Ekotto whose cross into the box was contested by Crouch and defender Nemanja Vidic. With the Serb unable to clear his lines the loose ball was met by Defoe, whose stunning overhead kick sent the ball zipping into the bottom corner. What a start for Spurs.

That, however, was as good as it got for the Lilywhites. They had been on the receiving end of Manchester United's trademark comebacks on their own turf before and this would be no different. Goals from the evergreen Ryan Giggs, Brazilian Anderson and a late strike from Rooney confirmed that Spurs still had plenty to do to match the big four.

The point was made again when Spurs travelled across London to face title challengers Chelsea. Defoe ended up on the peripheries of the game as the Blues powered to a 3-0 win at Stamford Bridge. Following a flying start to the season, Tottenham had suddenly lost two games in a row against the kind of teams they wanted to be competing with at the top of the table. However, there was no need for panic.

The third round of the League Cup took Spurs back up north to face Preston North End and, as at Doncaster in the previous round, the Londoners went goal crazy. Defoe scored with a header to make the score 2-0 but the night belonged to another England World Cup hopeful as Peter Crouch hit a hat-trick. Spurs ran out 5-1 winners and they continued their rich scoring form at home to newly promoted Burnley a few days later. This time Robbie Keane took the plaudits with four goals in a 5-0 victory.

As a result of his team-mates' excellent form, Defoe would be left on the bench for the first time in the league season. He had been in this situation before at Tottenham but this time he knew he was in no danger of being marginalised. In Harry Redknapp he had a manager who thought the world of him and with whom he shared a mutual trust. But that bond would be tested when they returned to Portsmouth.

Having tapped in his tenth goal of the season after Ledley King had opened the scoring, the hostile reception that Defoe had been receiving from the Pompey faithful eventually saw the striker boil over. His petulant and unnecessary stamp on Aaron Mokoena resulted in a straight red card and a public condemnation from his manager.

Redknapp, Crouch and Croatia midfielder Niko Kranjcar had also been given a hard time by the Fratton Park support but none of them had reacted. Defoe's ill-tempered and immature over-reaction to provocation earned him a dressing room dressing-down from the boss, who was clearly furious with his star striker's behaviour.

'I said to them all before the game that there was a lot of hype around this match and we've got to go out and play football,' fumed Redknapp. 'Anyone who's going to get carried away and start kicking and fighting people – that's not what we're here to do. Defoe can be like that. He has to learn to curb that. I couldn't have told him more. But he let himself down, he let us down as well. He could have cost us the game.'

Fortunately, he did not as Spurs clung on with ten men to win 2-1. Mokoena revealed that Defoe had apologised after the game but South African international was still angry with what his former team-mate had done. 'We know Jermain – he's a committed player. But that one was out of this world. Jermain has a bright future in the England squad, but doing what he did is embarrassing. It was a cheap shot.'

It was also a shot that would result in a three-match suspension. His absence would hurt Spurs as they lost the next two league games in a row: one a shock home defeat by Stoke, the other a dismaying 3-0 reverse at Arsenal. Defoe's return would come hand in hand with Tottenham's return to winning ways, as he set up Tom Huddlestone's goal in a 2-0 win over Sunderland at the Lane.

Fortunately Defoe's temper had not cost him his place in the England party, but his presence off the bench could not prevent a defeat to Brazil in a showpiece friendly at Doha's Khalifa International Stadium. However, after a tough period, Defoe was about to put things right in the best way possible. He was about to make history.

Forever etched into the memory of every Tottenham fan is the date 22 November 2009. Not only that, it is a date that will forever be associated with Jermain Defoe. After a start to the season in which Spurs had showcased their attacking credentials, the home fixture against Wigan Athletic was the kind of game they needed to win if they were to secure the fourth-place finish they craved. After Peter Crouch had given them a 1-0 half-time lead, all seemed to be going to plan.

But with the second half just a few minutes old, Tottenham went into overdrive. Inside seven minutes Defoe bagged a hat-trick – the second fastest in Premier League history. His first was finished from a Lennon cross, his second a cool finish after capitalising on a defensive slip and his third (just after

Wigan had pulled one back) a volley from eight yards out from another Lennon assist.

But it did not end there. Crouch fired in his second before Defoe cemented his place in football folklore with a thumping fourth goal and a fifth three minutes from time. He had scored five goals in one game – a Premier League record. Further goals from Kranjcar and David Bentley ensured the team's astonishing final score of 9-1 took its place in the top division's record books as well (it was only the second time a team had scored nine in a match).

Defoe's five-goal feat has only been matched by two men in the history of the Premier League. In 1995 Andy Cole scored five for Manchester United, 9-0 winners against Ipswich Town, and four years later Alan Shearer did the same as Newcastle recorded an 8-0 victory over Sheffield Wednesday. Now Jermain Defoe's name would be mentioned in the same breath as those two goalscoring legends of English football.

That in itself was a source of great pride for a man who had always been so open in his admiration for the finest strikers in the game. He was fortunate in being able to draw on the experiences of two other scoring greats of English football on the Spurs coaching staff, former Tottenham hotshots Clive Allen and 'Sir' Les Ferdinand, his partner for a short while at West Ham. In fact, the former had encouraged Defoe to change his boots before the game started, to wear his old boots instead of a brand new pair his sponsors had provided. It was a good thing he did.

Later Defoe revealed to the press just how much comparisons with the greats meant to him, and revealed how he still watches their goals on *YouTube*. But as he told *The Times*, it was not just their efforts that inspired Defoe to his five-goal salvo: 'All week before the game, every day, I was watching Thierry Henry goals.' And while one Arsenal legend was inspiring Defoe, another had been encouraging him all the way. Ian Wright had played with and mentored Defoe while at West Ham, and now the two were great friends.

'I speak to Wrighty all the time,' he continued. 'He just shouts on the phone. He doesn't speak, does he? He called after my five goals. He was screaming! The reason why he went mad was at the beginning of the season he said to me, "You know what, you'll get five in a game soon" – seriously, he did. He said, "Jay, you're the type of player who if you get five chances in a game you can score five."'

Five goals in a game is an incredible feat at any level, let alone the top of the English game, so it's not surprising that his achievement was hailed as 'a dream' by Defoe. Indeed he was convinced he had left his manager in shock. Well, Harry may not have been in shock, but he was certainly pretty taken with what he had seen and called on the England coach to take an even closer look. 'He's an amazing finisher. Wayne Rooney's fantastic – a complete all-round player – but as a finisher, Defoe is the best out there. I'm sure he'll go to the World Cup. Fabio will see the goals he's scored.'

The World Cup might have been providing the backdrop for Defoe's on-field exploits, but it was far more important in the short term to ensure Spurs did not tail off in their quest for the top four. After hitting the heights against Wigan, the next couple of games would prove frustrating for both player and club as they stuttered to a draw at fellow Champions League chasers Aston Villa and crashed out of the League Cup against Manchester United at Old Trafford.

Defoe failed to score in either game, and when he did get

back among the goals it would not be on one of the club's better days at Goodison Park. He had given his side the lead against Everton after being set up once more by Aaron Lennon, before defender Michael Dawson, another young man playing himself into contention for a World Cup place, headed in the second. However, the Toffees rallied and fought their way back to 2-2.

Just when it looked as though the points would be shared, Spurs were awarded an injury-time penalty. Up stepped Defoe, but his tame spot kick was easily saved by American goalkeeper Tim Howard. In the end, the points were indeed shared. Things did not get any easier for Spurs as they followed that disappointing outcome with a shock home defeat by struggling Wolves. If Tottenham were going to get a place in the top four, they were certainly going to have to do it the hard way.

Fortunately for Spurs, the result against Wolves appeared to be nothing more than a blip. Their next game against Manchester City, now vying for fourth place with Spurs after a summer of massive spending courtesy of their wealthy Arab owners, produced one of their finest performances of the season. Two goals from Kranjcar sandwiched another Defoe strike as he and Crouch linked up once again, the big man heading into his partner's path to nip past defender Kolo Toure and fire into the net. Tottenham's three-goal win underlined their Champions League credentials and piled the pressure on City, who sacked manager Mark Hughes just days after the defeat.

Defoe's good form ensured Spurs enjoyed a strong finish to 2009. His 15th goal of the season came against West Ham at White Hart Lane to seal a 2-0 win. That sent his team into the new year undefeated over the festive period, with four clean sheets in a row and in good shape for their best ever Premier League finish. They were certainly capable of it, according to Hammers boss Gianfranco Zola, who told the press: 'I know we lost, in my opinion, to one of the best teams in the country.'

Their good form in the league gave Spurs every confidence in knockout competition as well. They administered a crushing home defeat to Championship strugglers Peterborough in the third round of the FA Cup, Defoe scoring the third of Tottenham's four unanswered goals with a convincing finish from Welsh full-back Gareth Bale's cross. He could have scored more before eventually being replaced by Roman Pavlyuchenko but it mattered little.

The FA Cup proved to be something of a mixed bag for Defoe. After helping to see off Peterborough he and his team would take on a League One side in the next round. The drawback was that they were still taking on one of the biggest clubs in the country: Leeds United. As it turned out, two strikers with similar names would dominate the headlines for differing reasons at the Lane.

Defoe had the chance to give his team an early lead with a ninth-minute penalty. Unfortunately, his poor run from the spot continued as goalkeeper Casper Ankergren guessed right and saved. That was four saved penalties in a row for Defoe, and it prompted Harry Redknapp to question who would take them in the future with a typically frank assessment: 'I don't know if he's a great penalty taker, to be honest.'

Jermaine Beckford, on the other hand, stole the show. Having written himself into FA Cup history with a shock winner against Manchester United at Old Trafford in the previous round, he first levelled the score at 1-1 before Leeds were awarded a last-gasp penalty with the score at 2-1 to the Premier League side. Where Jermain had failed, Jermaine passed his test with flying colours, steering the ball into the net to take the tie back to Elland Road.

The lesson was not lost on Defoe: he knew he needed to be more clinical when it mattered. While his goalscoring form had been remarkable, he knew he had to put more chances in the back of the net when the pressure was on. His recent penalty misses had been costly, and if he was not going to score from the spot, he had to make sure his opportunities in open play were made to count. By the time the replay came round, Leeds would feel the full force of Defoe's resolution.

He was constant thorn in Leeds' side, creating chance after chance and continually popping up nightmare positions for the home defence. Eventually his persistence paid off with a fortuitous scuffed shot that somehow ended up in the top corner. No matter, though, as he grabbed two more that he did intend late in the second half. It was his third hat-trick of the season and Tottenham were heading to the fifth round. Redknapp again compared his star man to England team-mate Wayne Rooney, but was careful to remind Defoe that he was not perfect. 'He could have scored six because he had plenty of chances and he missed three that were probably easier than the ones he took,' said the manager. Defoe, to his credit, agreed.

In between the two games against Leeds, Defoe had continued his scoring streak with Tottenham's goal in a 1-1 draw at Birmingham. By the time the final whistle had gone at Elland Road after the cup replay, his total stood at 23 goals in all competitions. It was formidable scoring record, made all the more impressive by the fact it was only February –and by the fact that it was an identical haul to a certain Mr Rooney's tally.

'In terms of goals, it has all gone great this season,' enthused Defoe in an interview with the *Daily Telegraph*. 'Am I in the form of my career? In that sense, yes. I am playing with good players, I am happy and so, hopefully, if I keep working hard, I will get many more. I just want to keep it going.' As Rooney's fine achievements were matched blow for blow, momentum was gathering among pundits, journalists and fans for Defoe to be starting alongside the United striker in the England team. It spoke volumes that after the Leeds hat-trick, Defoe's signed match ball contained the following message from his friend Jermaine Jenas: 'I expect nothing less.'

As Tottenham's cup quest continued, so did Defoe's momentum. His crucial equaliser – a sweet left-footed strike helped on its way by a deflection – kept Spurs in the competition at Bolton Wanderers. They could have won but for yet another penalty miss, although this time it was Tom Huddlestone who picked up where Defoe had left off, watching in despair as Jussi Jaaskelainen made the crucial save.

While a draw and another replay was not the outcome Tottenham had been looking for, Defoe's latest strike had come on the back of a challenge from his manager to keep improving. 'He's a top class finisher when he has the opportunities,' said Redknapp before the Bolton game. 'But some days he must do that little bit extra to make it happen.' The striker had clearly been listening and wanted to do his best to repay his faith.

Indeed plenty would be said throughout February about Defoe's ability as the goals continued to flow. Former Arsenal,

Manchester United and England defender Viv Anderson was one of many in the game who were tipping him to fire England to World Cup glory come the summer. He told the *Mirror*: 'At international level you might only get three or four chances a game and having someone who can take one of those chances is a huge asset. And if Defoe is fit and playing as he is for Tottenham at the moment, he could be the one.'

Next to single him out was Tottenham's captain Ledley King. 'I think he's the best finisher in the country,' he told the same newspaper, 'and that's from anywhere, 25 yards and in. I've felt that for years. He's deadly. Jermain will always score goals. There are not too many forwards who can pick the ball up 25 yards out and still be a big threat. He can shift the ball and hit it from anywhere around the box. I've trained against him so I know he's a nightmare to play against, especially for big centre-halves, because the last thing you want is a little livewire around your knees!'

As if to oblige, Defoe took the field against Wigan at the JJB Stadium and proved everybody right. He was quickly becoming the Latics' worst nightmare, and it did not help that all the luck would go with him on the day. His goal just before the half hour, coming from Bale's cross, was quite clearly two yards offside. Wigan complained and Defoe himself looked towards the officials before celebrating, but the goal was given. 'Sometimes you get them, sometimes you don't,' mused Redknapp at the end.

However, he was also lucky to stay on the field after a nasty, lunging challenge on defender Gary Caldwell that left Wigan boss Roberto Martinez fuming that it was clearly a red card. Fortunately, some of the heat was taken out of the situation when he was wisely replaced by Pavlyuchenko, whose two late strikes sealed a comfortable win and deflated the Wigan fans' emotions somewhat.

With Tottenham very much involved in the race for fourth place, Defoe could concentrate on international matters at the beginning of March. His form had earned him a starting place for England's home friendly against Egypt at Wembley. Unfortunately, his lucky streak did not go with him. Despite threatening the African champions with his pace and movement, he never really looked like linking up effectively with Rooney and with England trailing 0-1 at half-time, he was replaced by a familiar face. Substitute Peter Crouch spared the home side's blushes with two goals in a 3-1 win.

Not Defoe's day for England, then, but he was still well on top of his game for Tottenham. Despite Crouch's exploits for England, Roman Pavlyuchenko had played his way into the Spurs manager's thoughts at his expense. Just as at Wigan some weeks earlier, the Englishman would score one and the Russian two against Blackburn Rovers as Tottenham's march to Europe continued apace. Ian Ridley in the *Mail on Sunday* summed up the situation perfectly: 'Good and bad news for England: Jermain Defoe is still scoring goals, but Peter Crouch can hardly get game time.'

That would soon change, however. Just a few days after the win over Blackburn came a blow that both he and Spurs had been dreading: Defoe pulled up in training with a torn hamstring. 'A massive loss at the worst possible time,' said Redknapp, as Spurs faced being without Defoe's goals for the best part of three weeks. Perhaps, in a World Cup year and with so much for Spurs to play for, they should have been grateful it was not more.

Fortunately, Defoe would not be missed as greatly as he had

been when he was suspended earlier in the season. Crouch would find his form to the relief of Spurs and England fans, and goals from Pavlyuchenko and Icelandic striker Eidur Gudjohnsen – on loan from Barcelona following Robbie Keane's temporary switch to Celtic in January – steered Tottenham to six more points in the league and the semi-finals in the FA Cup.

However, when Defoe returned as a substitute in early April for a league game at Sunderland, Spurs were put to the sword by the man he had effectively replaced. Darren Bent scored twice as Sunderland won 3-1 win, and it could have been even worse for Tottenham – Bent missed two penalties as well.

Things would get worse for Tottenham with Defoe's first start after his injury, in the cup semi-final at Wembley against his old club Portsmouth. Once more he, Crouch, Kranjcar and Redknapp would all feel the wrath of the fans who used to cheer them on as the cash-strapped south coast outfit – relegated from the top division just the day before – upset all the odds and battled to a shock 2-0 victory. But, as is so often the case in football, things can swing back your way very quickly indeed.

Tottenham had not beaten Arsenal in the league since 1999. The north London derby at White Hart Lane was another crucial meeting of the two great rivals and, not for the first time in Defoe's career, both sides had so much to play for. For Spurs, a first Premier League derby win in a decade would put them in the driving seat for the top four. For Arsenal, three points would keep them in the title race. With so much to gain and so much to lose, this particular derby was huge for players and fans alike.

The game got off to a blistering start as Spurs teenager

Danny Rose lashed the hosts into the lead with a spectacular volley from fully 30 yards out. The home fans were in raptures and, just a minute into the second half, they nearly took the roof off. Defoe was involved this time, using his strength to hold off defender Emmanuel Eboue and playing in Bale, who finished superbly. It was the perfect example of the 'little bit extra' that Redknapp wanted to see from his goalscorer-in-chief. Arsenal pulled a goal back late on but, thanks to the heroics of keeper Heurelho Gomes, Spurs clung on for a historic win.

The fans were ecstatic. Not only had Spurs beaten Arsenal in a league fixture for the first time in more than ten years, they had also effectively ended their rivals' hopes of winning the Premier League title. Added to that, they had seen their own team make a major statement about their Champions League credentials. They felt as though Spurs were ready for a crack at the best teams Europe had to offer and, having beaten one of them already, they were on cloud nine.

Just three days later another top team came to the Lane in the form of Chelsea, who were looking likely to win the title. But with Tottenham in this kind of form, another shock was on the cards. Just 15 minutes into the game Blues captain John Terry was adjudged to have handled in the box. Penalty. But who would take it? Spurs had missed enough spot kicks recently, but one man who had missed more than the rest would not be denied again. Defoe laid his personal demons to rest with a fantastic strike that almost broke the net. Aside from the goal, Defoe's performance was superb as he troubled one of the best defences in the division for all his 78 minutes on the pitch before being substituted. The watching Fabio Capello could not have failed to be impressed.

A second Spurs goal from Bale put the result beyond doubt, and though Frank Lampard netted a consolation, the hosts had done it again. They had shown their mettle against the team that would claim the title at the end of the season. Unfortunately for Defoe, the penalty would be his last goal of the season.

The next couple of games would see him substituted by Harry Redknapp, who offered the simplest of explanations. 'Why have I taken him off in recent matches? Because he wasn't playing very well.' Luckily for Spurs, his loss of form would not cost them. Peter Crouch was the hero, as his winning goal at Eastlands against Manchester City – the only team who could stop Spurs finishing fourth – ensured that Tottenham would be playing Champions League football in 2010/11.

It had been a fantastic season for Defoe, and a history-making one for Tottenham. He had scored 30 goals in club and national colours (24 for Spurs, six for England) and had made himself a mainstay in the England squad. Tottenham had reached the Champions League for the first time in their history and while their entire squad had performed admirably, they could not have done it without Defoe's goals. He had achieved one of his biggest aims, and now it was time to achieve another.

Following the end of the domestic season, Fabio Capello named his provisional squad of 30 players to be considered for the World Cup in South Africa. Defoe was one of six Tottenham players named, alongside Michael Dawson, Ledley King, Aaron Lennon, Tom Huddlestone and Peter Crouch. It was a superb achievement for the club, who had more players involved in the England squad than any other. If Defoe was to make it into the final 23 who would travel, he had to impress the coach in the two friendly matches that remained. Surely it was time to put his 2006 World Cup hell behind him for good

Chapter 10

In And Out Of Africa

The fact that Jermain Defoe had made it into Fabio Capello's initial 30-man squad came as little surprise to anyone who had paid attention the previous season. While there would be an element of doubt following what had happened four years earlier, when Defoe had been omitted from the final party for the untried Theo Walcott, the fact remained that he had enjoyed his best Premier League campaign in terms of goals scored, on-field performance and club success. In addition, he had become a mainstay in the Italian coach's thoughts throughout the qualification process and despite a slightly disappointing end to the season, there was absolutely no question that he fully merited his striker's spot in the group going to the pre-tournament training camp.

England were headed to Austria for high-altitude training as preparation for their games in South Africa, as their World Cup base at the Royal Bafokeng Sports Campus near

Rustenburg was some 5,000 feet above sea level. While in Austria the players would be assessed in training by the England management and coaching staff before returning home briefly for a friendly at Wembley against Mexico, then travelling back to Austria to play Japan. Following that game, Capello would whittle down the squad to his final 23 to represent England in the World Cup finals.

In terms of the competition for places, the coach had chosen five strikers in his provisional 30. Alongside Defoe were England regular and potential star of the tournament Wayne Rooney, who'd had a phenomenal season for Manchester United; Defoe's Spurs strike partner Peter Crouch, whose England record of 21 goals in 38 games made him a favourite for the final squad; Capello favourite Emile Heskey of Aston Villa, and Sunderland goal-getter Darren Bent – who, like Defoe, had his own 2006 demons to exorcise.

There was plenty of speculation about who should fill the striking spots in the final 23. Some critics felt that five strikers should have travelled to Germany in 2006 and would have supported taking all five forwards to South Africa. Other onlookers were convinced that Capello would again choose four strikers to travel and one would be left behind. While most people expected Bent to be the man to miss out again, Defoe knew he had to be at his very best to make sure of his seat on the plane.

And it was not just about positions up front that questions were being asked. There were issues all over the pitch to be resolved. Perhaps the biggest story of the pre-World Cup period was the decision made by Fabio Capello to tempt Liverpool defender Jamie Carragher out of international retirement. Despite the 2005 Champions League winner making it clear that he would not be talked into an England return, he agreed to the coach's request. It later emerged that Capello had also attempted to change the mind of Manchester United star Paul Scholes regarding his international future, but the former England midfielder chose to stay a former England midfielder.

There were also issues surrounding the goalkeeping situation. Although there was no doubt about who would travel to South Africa – David James of Portsmouth, West Ham's Robert Green and on-loan Birmingham City starlet Joe Hart were the only goalkeepers selected for the three available slots – nobody was sure who would be given the responsibility as England's number one. Despite criticism about who perhaps should have been picked – most notably from Blackburn manager Sam Allardyce, who could not believe his keeper Paul Robinson had been ignored on the back of perhaps his finest season – the three goalkeepers would have to battle it out in training and in the warm-up games in order to get the coveted position between the sticks.

As if all that was not enough, Capello had to think about his defensive and midfield options. At the back, new captain Rio Ferdinand was a fitness doubt, having had an injury-hit season, while Defoe's Spurs team-mate Ledley King's superb end to the season had been achieved despite constant knee problems. In midfield, holding player Gareth Barry was an injury doubt as well, and question marks remained over whether Capello should take an out-of-form Joe Cole or up-and-coming Manchester City star Adam Johnson. In addition, the unresolved question of whether or not Steven Gerrard and Frank Lampard could play together was set to resurface. By the time the Mexico fixture came around on a warm Monday evening at Wembley, there was a lot for the coach to think about.

There was also plenty for the players to be worried about. Not only were they playing for their places, they also knew the importance of making sure their final appearance on home soil before leaving for the best part of (hopefully) two months would be one to remember. The supporters wanted to give their heroes a rousing send-off and that meant the team had to give them something to cheer about. It is often the case that a friendly game is all about the performance, but this time the result seemed to matter just as much.

Defoe would occupy the place he had become used to on England duty – one of the substitutes – with his friend Crouch getting the nod to partner Rooney up front. Spurs were further represented by King at centre-half alongside Ferdinand. Green was given his chance in goal and the likes of Michael Carrick, Leighton Baines and James Milner were given the opportunity to stake their claims. However, with so much at stake, Defoe and the other subs knew there would be changes at some point, and their chance would come soon enough.

While all the focus at Wembley was on the England players, it seemed as though everybody in the ground had forgotten just how solid an outfit the Mexicans were. They impressed in possession and were the better team in the early stages of the game. Their pace and mobility were causing problems for a central defensive pairing whose recent injury problems were not helpful when it came to facing these qualities. Indeed England's heavy-leggedness at the back almost cost them when the visitors broke through, only for West Ham striker Guillermo Franco to fire just wide.

However, home advantage eventually told and when Gerrard's deep corner was headed back across goal by Crouch, King was on hand to head home from close range. What a story it had been so far for the Tottenham stalwart! The goal gave England the boost they needed and a second soon followed, with Crouch doubling Tottenham's presence on the scoresheet. He was almost certainly offside and looked to have handled the ball as he bundled it in, but two wrongs looked to have made a right as England went two goals to the good.

But Mexico were playing too well to get nothing from their first-half performance and Franco turned in a loose ball to reduce their arrears. It was no more than they deserved, having seen Green make a fine save when one-on-one with Arsenal youngster Carlos Vela and defender Carlos Salcido hit the post with a header. England went in 2-1 up at the break, perhaps fortunate to be leading against a side that looked to have exposed one or two cracks that would need repairing quickly if the Three Lions were to make an impact in South Africa.

Three changes were made at half time, with Hart replacing Green in goal, Carragher returning to the international arena in place of Ferdinand, and a Spurs-for-Spurs change with Crouch standing down for Defoe. The little man proved to be a bright addition, giving the Mexican defenders the same problems their strikers had given England, with his quick and nimble showing providing a different challenge to that of the physically imposing Crouch. However, for all Defoe's efforts the second half would be remembered for a sumptuous final goal from Liverpool defender Glen Johnson, who beat two men before curling home a superb left-footed strike from the edge of the box.

The score remained 3-1 to England at full time, and from a team perspective the job was well and truly done. They had achieved a morale-boosting victory – not just for themselves, but for the scores of fans packed into the national stadium and watching around the country. The players and coaching staff were given a rapturous send-off after the game with a lap of honour and the good wishes of all the supporters ringing in their ears. While Defoe had not been fortunate enough to play as great a part in proceedings as he would have wished, he knew his efforts had not gone unnoticed and he knew the team came first. Now he and the rest of the party would travel back to Austria for a final game against Japan that would make or break everybody's chances of making the final cut.

Having endured a tough test against a Mexican side keen to boost their own World Cup hopes, the England players were in for more of the same in Graz, against a Japanese side looking to establish their own credentials ahead of the world's biggest football competition. It was a shame, perhaps, that their opponents did not seem anywhere near as keen on the day.

Defoe was one of 11 England players who ended up not being used in this final warm-up fixture. Both he and Crouch would miss out as Rooney was partnered first by Bent and then by Heskey. It was as if those two men were playing off for the final place in the World Cup squad, although nobody – not least Defoe – could be sure of that.

However, it was probably for the best that Defoe would not be associated with such a listless England performance. Having fallen behind to a well-worked Marcus Tulio Tanaka goal, Capello's men needed two own-goals to turn the match back in their favour. Frank Lampard also missed a penalty and the team looked devoid of any kind of spark until Joe Cole was introduced at half-time. The performance had been poor but, if nothing else, England were at least in the winning habit. And now it was time for Mr Capello to break the news the entire country had been waiting for.

'I'm really sorry,' came the voice of Fabio Capello's right-hand man Franco Baldini down the phone. 'I'm afraid it's bad news.' Defoe could not believe his ears. Surely he was not to be overlooked again! Not after all he had been through four years earlier. Not after the emotional roller-coaster of a year he had been through both on the pitch and off it. This could not be happening to him. But not even the striker who had been through it all could believe what happened next.

'The bad news is you can't go on your holidays because you've got to go South Africa.' Defoe had been well and truly had. Of all the times to play a practical joke, Baldini had picked one heck of a moment. But there were no hard feelings from the Spurs man in the aftermath of the gag. He was going to the World Cup finals. Finally the boy from Beckton's dream had come true.

Having woken up at the crack of dawn, he had been 'terrified' all morning ahead of the moment that finally came at midday. 'It felt like such a long wait,' he admitted to the *Mirror*. 'I couldn't believe it – it was like having Simon Cowell on the phone. I'm so excited now; I just want to get out there.'

He was not the only member of the Defoe clan to be excited. His mum had seen it all before some four years earlier and was desperate not to see the same thing happen to her son again. 'The last few days have been a real déjà vu,' she told the *Mirror*. 'I'm remembering back to the last time, when at the last minute Jem didn't get picked. It was terrible – my heart broke for him. I couldn't understand why. Had he done something wrong? Was he not liked? But you can't think like that.

'I never cried in front of him because I didn't want him to think I was disappointed. I was just so sad for him. This time was the absolute opposite – I cried straight away. He rang on

Tuesday morning and shouted, "I'm in! I'm in!" and I burst into tears. I can't believe it. It's the proudest moment of my life.' But even Sandra knew this was only the beginning. 'Once the excitement about getting there is over, it's down to business,' she added. 'They've still got the hard work to do.'

But as Defoe knew only too well, in these situations one man's joy is another man's sorrow. Sunderland striker Bent had missed out and just as Defoe had been a surprise omission last time, there would be another shock on this occasion. Of all people, the young man who had taken Defoe's place in Germany in 2006 would miss out on the first ever World Cup finals in Africa: Capello had chosen to leave Theo Walcott at home. It later emerged that Walcott had not played to the tactics the strict Italian had wanted of him, and the coach had decided to pick Aaron Lennon and Shaun Wright-Phillips ahead of him. That was no consolation for the Arsenal youngster, but he had time on his side.

The other five players to miss out were Baines of Everton, Manchester City winger Johnson, West Ham's Scott Parker and Defoe's Tottenham team-mates Tom Huddlestone and Michael Dawson – although for the last-mentioned, disappointment would be short-lived. Just days before England's first game against the USA, team captain Ferdinand went down under an innocuous training-ground challenge from Emile Heskey and injured his knee. So serious was the damage in that accidental collision that Ferdinand's World Cup was over before it had begun. Steven Gerrard took the captain's armband and the England management moved quickly to summon Dawson to the squad as Ferdinand's replacement. It gave Spurs no fewer than five players in England's World Cup party – Lennon, King and Crouch joining Dawson and Defoe in South Africa.

However, in terms of the starting 11 for the opening match, the coach was giving nothing away. His regular practice was to name his team just a couple of hours before kick-off on the day of the match and that was not set to change for the summer. If anything could be taken from his choice of squad numbers, his naming of Crouch and Rooney as numbers nine and ten respectively suggested they could be his preferred strike pairing. Defoe was given number 19, leaving a place on the bench looking likely once again.

However, if the goalkeeping situation was anything to go by, David James' possession of the number one jersey did not make his position secure. Having struggled with a calf injury in the run-up to the tournament, there was every chance Capello would choose Robert Green, who had featured regularly throughout England's qualifying campaign. That said, rumours coming from the camp in Rustenburg just before the game suggested that Joe Hart would be given a shock chance having impressed in training.

There was also the chance to impress in one last friendly against local team Platinum Stars. Hart and Green would both feature again but it was up front that the attention was focused. Not only because Defoe scored England's opener with a smart finish from a Gerrard pass, but also because Joe Cole staked his claim for a place with a second goal and Wayne Rooney seemingly eased any concerns about his form and fitness with a third.

But that was a routine win against amateur opposition, and one or two dissenting voices around the camp were suggesting that the manager's policy of not revealing his team until the last minute was unhelpful for the players. The accusation was already looking like a potential stick with which to beat the head coach should things not go England's way. Although when the first game did come around, the talking would eventually stop.

England's first game in Group C, against the USA, was one they were expected to win. Despite the Americans' consistent improvements over the past year, including a Confederations Cup final appearance just 12 months earlier, the fact remained that England's experienced players were stronger. The choices that Capello made included Green to start in goal, King to start at centre-back instead of Ferdinand and James Milner to start on the left of midfield, pushing Gerrard into the middle alongside Frank Lampard as Gareth Barry was not quite ready to return. Unfortunately, all three inclusions would fail to have the desired effect.

It seemed as though everything was going to plan for England in the early stages. Defoe had been left on the bench as expected with Heskey preferred to partner Rooney, as he had done so well throughout qualification. The decision paid off almost immediately when, just three minutes into the game, the target man's flick-on found Gerrard clear in the box to slide the ball expertly beyond US keeper Tim Howard. England's 2010 World Cup finals had got off to a flying start.

But that was as good as it got for the Three Lions on the night. After half an hour, Milner, having struggled against America's pacey right-back Steve Cherundolo, was replaced by Shaun Wright-Phillips. At half-time Ledley King was forced off with a new injury concern, this time to his groin. Sandwiched in between was one of the most inexplicable errors ever made by goalkeeper Green.

Shortly before the break, a long range shot from Fulham midfielder Clint Dempsey looked to be sailing harmlessly straight towards the West Ham custodian. But despite positioning himself correctly, Green somehow allowed the controversial Jabulani ball to spill from his grasp and squirm agonisingly over the line. After all the talk before the game about who should play in goal, this awful moment ensured the debate would rage again.

England never recovered. They created chances in the second half but failed to score. Perhaps their best opportunity fell to Heskey, but he could only fire straight at Howard when clean through. His lack of confidence in front of goal was there for all to see, but Defoe could only look on from the bench. There was nothing he could do, and when Heskey was eventually replaced, it was Peter Crouch who replaced him. Defoe would have to wait for his World Cup to get started. It looked as though England would have to wait for theirs to start as well, as the game ended in a disappointing 1-1 draw.

Realistically, the result was not a total disaster for England. The USA were the strongest team they would face in the group stages and the games against Algeria and Slovenia would surely not be as tough. The problem was the manner of the result. A poor goalkeeping error and a team selection that had not done the job had left England facing an uphill battle and question marks were already hanging over both players and management.

As a result there was renewed speculation about who would play against Algeria, and one of the names mentioned in the frame for a starting slot was that of Defoe. England were missing something up front and needed a spark. While Heskey and Crouch offered a towering physical presence, Defoe offered pace and a direct approach that was needed with England looking for the win that would get their tournament back on track.

Unfortunately Mr Capello did not see it that way, and he plumped for Heskey again. He did make a change in goal, however, with James returning to fitness to replace the hapless Green. But in terms of things to note, that was about it. If England's performance against the USA was not up to scratch, their effort against Algeria was nothing short of dismal. When Defoe did eventually enter the fray in the 74th minute for his World Cup finals debut, the game had well and truly gone stale. He offered plenty in the way of a threat to the North African defence, but nobody else in England colours could bring anything to the table.

It was the drabbest of goalless draws and it saw the Three Lions booed off the pitch by the fans who had sacrificed so much to make it to South Africa. Their situation was not helped when Wayne Rooney criticised those fans for their reaction in an angry outburst directly to a television camera. Something needed to change quickly if England were even going to make it out of the group – let alone reach the latter stages.

That point, it seemed, was not lost on the players. With the pressure mounting and the scrutiny on the camp seemingly unbearable, disgraced former captain John Terry appeared to call the players for a crisis meeting in a passionate press conference after the game, insisting they get whatever issues they had off their chest. He further explained that he and a number of other players in the squad had got together for a beer – after reportedly having pleaded with the England management – and discussed what they felt had gone wrong.

However, he then went on to suggest that Fabio Capello should change his team selection – specifically to include Terry's Chelsea team-mate Joe Cole. This was a step too far. Terry was forced to apologise and insisted that he was fully behind the manager. Unfortunately, that did little to calm the inevitable media storm that followed, suggesting that Terry had tried to reassert himself by staging some kind of mutiny in the camp. This was perhaps as unhealthy a backdrop to a crucial game as Capello could ever have encountered. But whether pressure from the squad, the media and the supporters on the outside had had any effect or not, there were changes for the Slovenia game. But not the change the former skipper suggested.

The 'crisis meeting' never materialised. Instead, as expected, the manager sat his players down to watch a DVD of the Algeria disaster, highlighting where they had gone wrong before moving on to prepare for the next game. With only one goal scored so far in the tournament, and none from his strikers, Capello knew England needed goals. The Slovenia match was a must-win game, and to win you need to score. Wayne Rooney's partner for England's final group game knew exactly how to do that.

Wearing the number 19 shirt made famous by another Tottenham hero, Paul Gascoigne, in the 1990 World Cup, Jermain Defoe took to the field as the man upon whom English hopes were to be placed. Behind him was Matthew Upson, who had come into the team for his first appearance of the tournament in the absence of the suspended Carragher and the injured King, and Milner in place of the misfiring Lennon. These amendments to the side, however, did not ensure the brightest of England starts to the game. Indeed they only created one clear-cut chance in the first quarter of the game. Although for one man, one chance was all it needed.

With 23 minutes on the clock, a quick free-kick taken by Terry saw the ball moved quickly to the waiting Milner on the right wing via Johnson, Lampard and Barry. Milner took a couple of touches to steady himself and fired a teasing cross into the six-yard area. For many players the pressure of finishing such a crucial chance would be too much to handle. But for Defoe, this part of the pitch was where he could let instinct take over. He darted in front of his man and flicked the ball into the net on the volley. 'In to pounce where and when it most matters,' shouted BBC commentator Guy Mowbray to the watching millions. It summed Defoe up in a nutshell.

His 12th England goal proved to be enough. The Three Lions missed their share of chances – even Defoe could and should have grabbed another as well as having one more ruled out for offside – and Slovenia might well have snatched an equaliser but for some heroic England defending (from the much-maligned Terry, no less), but it was enough. Just. England had crept through to the next round by the skin of their teeth, and they had done it thanks to Defoe making yet another of his dreams come true. He had scored a goal for England in the World Cup finals.

'I'm lost for words,' he enthused after the game. 'What a moment! You can imagine the calls and texts I've been getting asking. "How does it feel?" As a young lad, you dream about doing it one day. I was focused before the game and we won, which is the most important thing.'

Once again his family was the first thing on his mind after the year they had been through. 'Mum was crying even before the game,' he told the media. 'She told me she had all the family round which put a bit more pressure on me to play well but it was great to score for them. I've always kept the faith and kept working hard. My mum always said to me if you work hard you get rewarded and I definitely got my reward.'

He was not short of praise from his team-mates. Frank Lampard said of England's goal hero immediately after the match: 'He's a goalscorer. He's done it everywhere, he's been around and he's continued to do it today. It's not easy to come in when you haven't really played. He had a few minutes against Algeria, but has not really been involved. People expect goalscorers to come in and score instantly and it doesn't always happen like that. He's done it because he's very sharp and he was in the right place.'

The plaudits did not stop there. The English press were all over Defoe's glorious contribution to the team's campaign. Matt Barlow described the striker as a 'livewire' in the *Daily Mail*, while the same newspaper's former England player-cum-columnist Jamie Redknapp wrote: 'There isn't another player in the England squad with the ability to move and finish like Jermain Defoe.' The red-top tabloids were also full of admiration with Defoe's celebration of his goal the dominant picture on the front page of both the *Sun* and the *Mirror*, whose headline read simply: 'JERMAINIA!' The latter newspaper's excitement was certainly understandable – after all, Defoe had written a column for them during the past season.

Defoe's glamour model girlfriend Roxy Townsend was also impressed. 'He was so happy and excited,' she said. 'He said it was the best thing that had ever happened to him. I thought he was going to explode with excitement. I just kept saying, "Well done!" and told him how happy he'd made people back home in England.' Indeed it looked as though he had made plenty of people very happy indeed – despite the country being in the grip of recession. Indeed the Centre of Economics and Business Research suggested that the British economy would have lost a further £1.2 billion had England gone out of the

World Cup finals at such an early stage.

But this was not about the money. It was all about England progressing in the World Cup. The coach was delighted with his team, claiming that the performance against Slovenia was what he had been waiting for. 'This is the spirit that I remember when we played in the qualification games,' he said. 'I am really happy with the performance of the team. We played together, fought together and I am really, really happy for the result.' And the secret, according to Fabio? 'Yesterday evening they drank beer before the game.' Could John Terry have been right all along? Capello did not go that far, but he made clear there was no problem with Terry or indeed with any of the England players. The noises coming from the camp suggested they were ready for anybody.

As it happened, they would need to be. Winning the group would have allowed England a potentially easier run to the semi-finals with likely games against Ghana and Uruguay to follow. However, a last-gasp winner from USA talisman Landon Donovan earned the Americans a win against Algeria to push England down to second in the group. Now any hopes of reaching the last four and equalling their best World Cup since 1966 would rest on beating Argentina – but only if they could get past even older foes: Germany.

It was certain to be one of the toughest tests any England team had faced. The footballing history between the two nations was more than enough to whet the nation's collective appetite, with England's finest hour in 1966 being followed by agonising defeats on penalties in 1990 World Cup and Euro '96 semi-finals, then a 5-1 victory against the Germans in Munich in 2001. But as their rebuilding continued, Germany now looked a dangerous prospect. Despite a surprise defeat in their middle group game against Serbia, they had seen off Australia with a thumping 4-0 win and Ghana by a single goal to top the group.

Not only that, it was a different Germany to the machine of popular memory. This team continued its open, attacking style of the 2006 World Cup finals, but it had suffered injuries to crucial players, including their influential captain Michael Ballack. This squad was far less experienced, but featured many impressive youngsters from its successful European Under-21 Championship winning team of 2009 that, coincidentally, had hammered England in the final. What they lacked in years, they more than made up for in technique, pace and style. This Germany team was fearless.

But that did not stop England going into the game with an air of confidence. They had finally managed to win and they had done so with an improved performance. The players readily accepted they had not been at their best, but they felt they were getting there with every passing day in South Africa. Defoe was no different, and did his best to sum up the mood in the camp in a pre-match press conference ahead of the meeting in Bloemfontein.

'It's important for the players not to think about the history between the two sides,' he warned. 'Just approach it like any other game – be confident and bright and just play the way we played against Slovenia. We have to be confident, believe we can win the game, and I am sure we can.' He admitted that perhaps the team would have been happier facing Ghana but the striker was convinced the mood in the camp could prepare them for any opposition.

'This is definitely the biggest match of my career,' he added. 'Every game is a big game but I'm really looking forward to this one and if called upon I'll be ready.' And would he be ready if the unthinkable happened and once again a penalty shootout would be needed? Would he take a penalty despite his mixed record from the spot over the previous season? '100 per cent,' came the instantaneous response.

But for all the positive thinking, there was no hiding from the fact that England were nowhere near as ready for this test as their opposition. Before the game, Germany legend Franz Beckenbauer suggested that England would be less than happy to have finished second in a group they should have won and ended up facing a German side high on confidence. How right he would prove to be.

Defoe retained his place for the last-16 encounter, as did everyone else who had started the game against Slovenia. For the first time in his tenure as England boss, Fabio Capello used the same starting 11 for two games running. Unfortunately, however, the game was an absolute disaster for all in England red that day.

Germany were all over their opponents from the first whistle but when they eventually took the lead on 19 minutes it was with the most basic of goals. A huge punt up the middle from goalkeeper Manuel Neuer was completely misjudged by both Terry and Upson, allowing striker Miroslav Klose in to slot beyond James. Just after the half-hour mark it was two as England were left hopelessly exposed at the back for Lukas Podolski to double the advantage.

Upson pulled a goal back with a header just a few minutes later before England's World Cup campaign took a turn for the absolute worst. A probing run by Defoe led to the ball breaking loose on the edge of the Germany penalty area and Lampard was on hand to execute a delightful chipped effort.

It hit the underside of the crossbar, bounced down at least a foot over the line before bouncing out again and being cleared by the opportunistic Neuer. Both referee and linesman managed to miss it, despite every other soul in the ground seeing the ball go into the goal. Instead of going in level at half-time, England remained 1-2 down. 'When things like that happen you definitely think it's not meant to be,' said Defoe in the aftermath of the game. It was something of an understatement.

Things got even worse as England chased the game. Two goals on the break from Thomas Muller exposed England's defensive frailties and the tactical weaknesses that many had feared before the tournament had begun. After the fourth goal, with 20 minutes to go, Defoe was replaced by Heskey – a curious decision by Capello given how few goals the Aston Villa man had scored all year, for club or country. For Germany, the 4-1 result was the perfect revenge for 1966 and continued a passage through the tournament that would see them lose a semi-final to eventual winners Spain and finish third overall. But for England? The inquest would begin.

It seemed everything and everyone was to blame – players, manager, coaching staff, altitude, tiredness, the new World Cup ball – and the press wasted no time in making their feelings known. The overall mood seemed to be summed up in brief by Steve Howard in the *Sun*: 'Men against boys – and the boys won. And all in front of 25,000 heroically loyal fans who, long before the end, were as humiliated as the players who perpetrated the foul deed. Yet it's now so inevitable, it's not even depressing. Apart from the scale of the defeat. As for Fabio Capello, should he contemplate staying on after this he must have a death wish.'

The players were not spared either, including the same Defoe who had been so vociferously lauded after the Slovenia game. The speed with which things could change was exemplified by Nick Miller's assessment of the striker's performance on *Football365.com*. He described Defoe as 'utterly, utterly anonymous' and continued, 'when a team performs this poorly elsewhere, they require someone with more wit, touch and appreciation of teamwork to contribute. Defoe is not that man.' The words were harsh, but Defoe was not the only player to be on the receiving end. In fact, compared with what was said about other more senior players and the coach, he got off lightly. At least he had contributed something during the competition that had made the fans happy – if only for a few days.

But while the press continued to pillory the players for their lack of commitment and the manager for his lack of ability, Defoe was one of the first England players to leap to the defence of both parties. There were suggestions that Capello had lost the dressing room due to his strict approach to discipline, but the Spurs striker insisted there was nothing but respect from the players towards their coach, and he insisted they would all back him to stay on.

'Maybe it's because so many players have taken on so much pressure to live up to expectations that it affected their normal game,' read his column in the *Mirror*. 'You have to remember that the strict regime is the way the manager prefers to do things. His CV is second to none and he has won titles and trophies with four top European clubs and some fantastic players that way. For me personally, he gave me an opportunity and I'd like to think that I took it in that Slovenia game. And I'd like to think, despite what is being said, that he has the respect of the players.'

He added: 'I can understand the level of anger and frustration that we as England players have returned home to. I accept it has been a bitterly disappointing World Cup campaign from a group of players of whom everyone expected so much. Personally I wish I could have done more to help the country than just the goal against Slovenia. I remain convinced that had I played in the earlier two games we would have got off to a better start than we did. And that's why it hurts so much to hear people saying we don't care. I care. I care passionately. I won't have anyone telling me I don't have pride in pulling on an England shirt. Pride in scoring goals for my country. Pride in representing my family, my club and the people that have had faith in me all my life.'

Defoe was not the only one to show he cared. Capello insisted he would not resign as England coach and, after some deliberation, the FA agreed to keep him in charge. The World Cup had certainly not gone to plan, but the Italian was determined to put things right for the future. And so was Defoe. Indeed the future looks immeasurably bright for one of the few England players to return from South Africa with any credit.

On the pitch, Jermain Defoe has plenty to look forward to. His international stock is certain to rise, having been the only England striker to find the net in four games at the World Cup finals. That achievement in itself must make him a crucial part of England's immediate future, especially under Fabio Capello. While the Italian remains in charge he will be fully aware now of what the Spurs star is capable of, if he was not already.

On an individual basis the achievement itself meant so much to Defoe. His entire professional career has been aligned to a burning desire to play, and score, in a World Cup finals. To shine on the greatest stage the sport has to offer. He has done that, and he has managed it before his 30th birthday. Many players do not even manage such a feat in their entire career. There is still at least one more World Cup left for the striker, who has yet to reach his peak.

Despite the disappointment of South Africa, there is plenty for Defoe to look forward to in an England shirt. With a 2012 European Championship qualifying campaign about to begin, he is sure to be one of the first names listed in the initial squads should he maintain his club form. And looking at the continual improvements in his game season on season, there is every chance that that is set to continue in the Premier League.

Defoe is at a club where he is happy and, after some years of moving between teams and facing questions about his commitment following the episodes at Charlton, West Ham and Portsmouth, he looks to be truly settled at Tottenham. He is loved by the fans and he is loved by the manager. He has reached the pinnacle of his career under Harry Redknapp and with the manager committing to a contract extension that will keep him at the club until at least 2013, the duo look set to keep their strong relationship going.

What a time it is to play for Tottenham. Even though Defoe has achieved his dreams at international level, there are now so many new opportunities at White Hart Lane. He has played in European competition before but never in the Champions League. With Spurs he now has that chance. He can go on to show that he is able to shine in the biggest and most lucrative club competition in world football. Perhaps winning it is a step too far for Tottenham at this stage – especially as they must qualify for the group stage first – but the chance to appear in the competition proper and rub shoulders with the likes of Barcelona, Real Madrid and Inter Milan is one that is truly befitting of the best players around.

Even in the domestic game there is still so much left for Defoe to achieve. He will be desperate for his luck to change in domestic cup competitions and while Spurs are competing at the right end of the Premier League table, there will always be the chance to play at Wembley again and pick up a winner's medal. And in the Premier League the levels of expectation directed at Tottenham will be high. They have achieved their best ever finish with the league in its current format and will want to do even better next time – even if Manchester City are intent on spending their many, many millions to take a place among the elite as well.

Admittedly, however, things off the pitch are still not quite perfect for Defoe. Following his arrest in 2009 for an alleged motoring offence (he is accused of using a mobile phone while driving), a date has been set for him to stand trial at magistrates' court. Defoe's legal representative has insisted a 'not guilty' verdict will be the outcome. One hopes Defoe will be able to put this episode behind him as he has done with other indiscretions that have led to his private life coming under the sort of scrutiny he is keen to avoid.

But forward movement in his personal life will always be a strong possibility with mum Sandra watching his every move. His reputation as something of a ladies' man and a stereotypical well-paid English footballer will forever be kept in check as long as she is around, as she explained in an interview with the *Mirror*: 'I want him to settle down with a nice, homely girl. I don't care anything about her background as long as she loves Jermain for him, not for what she can get.

'The lifestyle doesn't put Jermain in a good light. I think that's his vice really. And although I don't know firsthand what happens in these nightclubs, I've heard the girls physically stand around, hanging around waiting for whatever. I just want him to find a good girl. A girl I can embrace and say, "My daughter-in-law," someone with good family values and respect for herself. That's not asking too much, is it? When the right time comes with the right girl, he'll do it. He'll settle.'

Sandra is thinking even further ahead for her golden boy, even as far as when he finishes playing. Television could come calling after she revealed one more talent that very few realised he had. 'He's a fantastic dancer,' she smiled. 'He's got all these caps and trophies for football but he has one for dancing too. He won a prize for the whole of his school when he was little. I was so proud of that – we've got the trophy in a cabinet with his football ones. I've always said if he didn't make it as a footballer, he would have been a professional dancer. If he could get on *Strictly Come Dancing* or something when he retires from football it would be good. He's very much in tune with music, he always has been.'

There is still so much left for Defoe to achieve. From breaking records as a teenager at Bournemouth, to setting Upton Park alight with West Ham, to scoring on almost every debut he has made at club and international level, to his astonishing five-goal haul for Tottenham, his individual accolades have propelled him to the forefront of the national game and cemented his place in English football history. But as the commonly held belief in football goes, you can only be judged a true great when you have the winners' medals to back it up. If ever there was a right place and a right time to win trophies, it is at this point in his career with Tottenham Hotspur. Both club and player are on the up. The League Cup and FA Cup are certainly within reach. As far as the Premier League and Champions League go, you have to be in to win – and Tottenham are. Just one of those trophies may well suffice for Defoe. And the *Strictly Come Dancing* title for his mum too, of course.